America's GREATEST ROAD TRIP!

America's
GREATEST
ROAD TRIP!

KEY WEST TO DEADHORSE

9,000 MILES ACROSS BACKROAD USA

TOM COTTER
MICHAEL ALAN ROSS

motorbooks

ACKNOWLEDGMENTS

Lots of people helped make this trip possible, and we truly thank all those who believed in us. Said Deep and Diane Southall at Ford Motor Company were the first to sign up. Then my colleagues at Hagerty, McKeel Hagerty and Doug Clark, asked where to sign. Those two sponsors made it easier to convince our new friends at Airstream—Mollie Hansen, Jackie Doseck, and Dicky Riegel, to loan us our home on wheels for a few months.

To give our "rig" a unique look, friend Dwight Knowlton designed an amazing graphics package that never failed to be our conversation starter. And Rich Dagenhart did a great job printing up those decals. Richard Griot of Griot's Garage in Tacoma, Washington, reached out and offered to make our dirty rig clean again—his crew fully detailed it—before it became very dirty again.

Then there were the people who took us in (some literally), Jack Baldwin and Katherine dePoo; Ant Matsuda and Toni Pinto; Brian Weller; Mike Holtzclaw; Ann and Peter Keohan; Bill, Marlyn and Marwin Cotter; Mark Greene (Cars Yeah) and wife Jill; Jim Sfetko and Penny Sharp; Robyn Pass Handy; Emma Rieves (Summit Coffee); Trevor Gowan; Julie Gu; Kevin Fisher; and Brian and Kris Laine.

Plus the guy who has made all these books possible, my Motorbooks editor, publisher, and friend Zack Miller. I hope you'll allow me to write a few more! And Steve Roth, also of Motorbooks, helped us navigate the new world of social media before, during, and after the trip was over.

And of course our wives, Pat Cotter and Danielle Botros.

ABOUT THE AUTHOR AND PHOTOGRAPHER

TOM COTTER has been involved in numerous automotive and racing industries over his career. Working his way from mechanic and auto salesman to heading the PR department at Charlotte Motor Speedway, Cotter then formed his own racing and automotive PR and marketing agency, Cotter Group. His agency represented top clients in NASCAR, IndyCar/CART, drag racing, and road racing. Cotter has written biographies for the legendary Holman-Moody race team, Tommy Ivo and Dean Jeffries, but is best known for his series of barn-find books, including *The Cobra in the Barn*, *50 Shades of Rust*, and *Barn Find Road Trip*. Cotter hosts *The Barn Find Hunter* Youtube series, which is sponsored by Hagerty. He sits on the Advisory Board of McPherson College's Auto Restoration program and is a member of the Road Racing Driver's Club. He lives with his wife, Pat, Briggs (dog), Button (cat), and his car collection in Davidson, North Carolina.

Above: Photographer Michael Alan Ross (left) and author Tom Cotter.

MICHAEL ALAN ROSS' photography has been featured in advertising and editorial work for magazines and is part of corporate photography collections in the United States and in Europe. His vast knowledge of automotive design and his ability to create a visually stimulating image combined with Michael's masterful composition is the key to his tremendous success.

The extensive list of Michael's prestigious clients is indicative of the caliber of his work. They include: automotive manufacturers Porsche, Porsche Design, Polestar, Audi, Jaguar, Hagerty and magazines such as *Christophorus*, *Road & Track*, *EVO*, *Porsche Panorama Magazine*, *Excellence Magazine*, *000 Magazine*, *Hot Rod*, and *Rodder's Journal*.

Michael has just finished his sixth book with Motorbooks (Quarto Publishing) and author, Tom Cotter, under such titles as *Rockin' Garages*, *Barn Find Road Trip*, *Route 66 Barn Find Road Trip*, *Motor City Barn Finds*, *Ford Model T Coast to Coast*, and their latest book, *America's Greatest Road Trip*.

Their collaboration and friendship has afforded him a new level of appreciation for the open road and the great "finds" along this beautiful country of ours.

Michael has painstakingly and meticulously documented their adventures from rock star interviews to being bitten by junk yard dogs and everything in between...

As Tom Cotter likes to proclaim, "nobody sweats the details like MAR".

In response, Michael quips, "no matter what happens, a good cup of coffee and a good sense of humor" are the main ingredients for success!"

Dedicated to the brave people of Ukraine.

America's GREATEST ROAD TRIP!

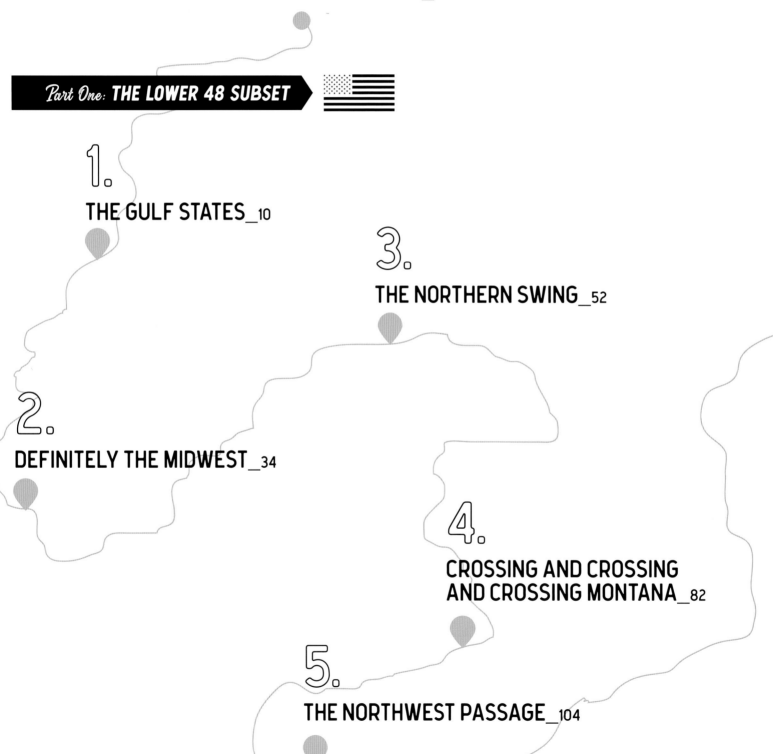

INTRODUCTION

In the early 1960s, retired race driver Carroll Shelby wanted to build his own sports car to beat his rival, Ferrari, on the racetrack. The problem: Carroll didn't have any money. But he was one heck of a salesman.

He saw that AC Cars in England built a lightweight, good-handling car called the Ace, but it lacked sufficient power to challenge Ferrari. Closer to home, Ford Motor Company had just introduced a compact V-8 that produced good power and would slot into the Ace's narrow chassis.

Shelby hoped AC Cars would supply him its Ace minus an engine, and he simultaneously hoped Ford would supply him engines. But that pesky detail remained: he had no money—no matter.

He convinced Ford that he had AC in his back pocket to supply him with cars. Then he visited AC and convinced them that he had Ford in his back pocket to supply engines. Of course, neither story was true.

The result of Shelby's sleight of hand was the AC Cobra, one of the most famous and successful racing sports cars of all time.

I relate this bit of history because I found myself in a similar situation as I was organizing the trip described in this book.

I'd been thinking about a road trip from Florida to Alaska for years, always wondering about the most appropriate vehicle for the journey. I considered a few options: my resto-mod 1939 Ford Woody; a 1967 Shelby GT350; a car from Craigslist that I would buy in Miami and sell in Fairbanks; a cheap 1980s Corvette; a Volkswagen camper; and a host of others. But I never advanced beyond the dream stage.

Then, in the fall of 2021, it hit me: "What if I took the car out of the equation?" In other words, what if I wasn't looking for vintage car at all, but an appropriately modern vehicle?

A Bronco! Bingo! A 2021 Outer Banks edition manufactured by an iconic American company, Ford. Plus, it was the hottest new vehicle on the market. My initial conversations with Ford

Below: Carroll Shelby at the wheel of a very early Shelby-Cobra 260 in Venice, California, October 7, 1962. (Photo by Bernard Cahier/ Getty Images)

were inconclusive though. "We sell every unit we can build," they told me. In other words, "Why would we lend one to you?"

So I put on my Stetson, in homage to Carroll Shelby, and tried again.

"But I have Airstream and Hagerty sponsorship in my back pocket," I told Ford.

Then I approached Airstream with my adventure idea. I heard a similar refrain from them: "As you can imagine, we are approached constantly by authors and filmmakers who want to use our trailers for their projects, but our production is already three years behind. Still, having partners like Ford and Hagerty is pretty strong. . . ."

The third piece of the puzzle, Hagerty, was an easier sell. I was at the Amelia Island Concours d'Elegance in 2022, signing copies of my book, *Secrets of the Barn Find Hunter* with McKeel Hagerty, who wrote the book's introduction. When I revealed my Key West–to–Deadhorse road trip idea to him, he said, "We're in!" I worked closely with Doug Clark, McKeel's right-hand man, and his team to make the dream come true.

Ultimately it came together like clockwork, but it was certainly nerve rattling along the way.

You now hold in your hands the final piece of the America's Greatest Road Trip puzzle. All I had to do was tell the publisher, "Hey, I have Ford, Airstream, and Hagerty in my back pocket."

And like Shelby, I wound up with a couple of winners. Ford graciously loaned us a 2021 Outer Banks Bronco four-door equipped with a 2.7-liter Ecoboost engine and a hardtop. The Bronco's towing capacity was rated at a maximum of 3,500-pounds, which worked out well, because Airstream makes only one trailer under that weight, the Basecamp 16X. When I asked the PR folks at Airstream whether two guys could survive in a 16-foot trailer for eight weeks, they said, "Yes, but you're going to get real tired of each other."

Hagerty contracted my friend, artist and author Dwight Knowlton, to design unique and informative adhesive vinyl graphics that would act as a rolling billboard, a conversation starter at gas stops and campgrounds. At the trip's conclusion, the decals could simply be pealed off.

Besides documenting the people we met and the places we visited, you'll also be treated to reviews of some of the more memorable coffee shops we frequented. My coffee-snob codriver, MAR, will give you his My Morning Mug impressions.

Enjoy the ride!

THE ROOTS OF A ROAD TRIP

Key West to Deadhorse had been fermenting in my head for years. I didn't need much reason to travel to Alaska, a state I love visiting. As is my style, I originally considered driving from Key West to the Arctic Circle in some sort of vintage vehicle. I considered a mid-1980s Corvette, a car that is equal parts underappreciated, reliable, and unexpected in the Alaskan outback. I also thought about buying some sort of interesting car on Craigslist in Miami, driving it to Alaska, then selling it on the same platform once I made it to Fairbanks, writing about my experience along the way.

Around 2017, I began to plot the trip with my buddy Woody Woodruff. Woody was an interesting guy, a Vietnam veteran, original owner of a 1967 Shelby GT350, and someone who'd drop anything to help me. In other words, my best friend in the world. Without giving me any warning, he once took a train from Charlotte to Albuquerque so he could help me drive my woody to Chicago in order to meet a deadline.

Woody was also the main culprit in the infamous Fig Newton Fiasco, which I will detail later.

When I first brought up the trip, Woody had been diagnosed with pancreatic cancer but was responding well to treatment. He was eager to do a lot of living while he could. We schemed about driving his Shelby Mustang to Alaska, stopping at veterans' hospitals along the way to bring attention to his form of cancer.

Then Woody's health took a sharp turn for the worse and he passed. My road trip plans were scrapped.

Still I knew Woody would have wanted the trip to go forward, so I began plotting again in his honor. Everyone who met Woody loved him. He was an unselfish guy, a terrific listener, and a quick friend to strangers.

I decided to refocus the journey to one that would honor the working people and regular folks America we'd meet along the way. We would travel two-lane America, meeting the people who live away from the interstates and metropolises, the ones who are busy living their lives, not making noise.

With all the daily vitriol coming from mainstream media—social and otherwise—I hoped that, by the time we reached the Arctic Ocean, we would be pleasantly surprised by the positive attitudes and common concerns of our fellow Americans.

I took the vehicle out of the equation—sort of. Instead of documenting the trials and tribulations that come with driving a vintage vehicle 7,000 miles (11,265 kilometers), we would instead drive a reliable, backroads-appropriate vehicle, keeping our eyes open for human interest stories as we encountered them.

But, like Popeye, "I yam what I yam": I just can't stop looking for and writing about cars. There was no way I could put my obsession with four-wheeled things in the back seat and ignore whatever cars came our way.

1.

THE GULF STATES

Oppoiste, top left: Friends and Key West residents Jack Baldwin and Kathryn dePoo invited us to experience Keys cuisine at an authentic dockside restaurant, Hogfish Bar & Grill. It was the ideal way to taste local food as well as learn about life at the end of the road from Kathy, a Conch, and Jack, a newbie.

Opposite, top right: Because MAR spends most of his time on the other side of the camera, I thought I'd include this photo of the world's best codriver as we spent two days in Key West as tourists. We'd soon turn our Bronco and Airstream north and begin the longest point-to-point drive in North America.

Opposite, bottom: Jack is a rather unusual Key West resident—he's a car enthusiast. After owning a slew of muscle cars and sports cars, this is his current ride, a 1963 Studebaker Avanti. The car's design and its color seem to work well with Key West's architecture and vibe. As we ate dinner, both diners and patrons came out to inspect his beautiful set of wheels.

WASTING AWAY IN MARGARITAVILLE

We'd been in Key West for fewer than twenty-four hours and had already heard Jimmy Buffett's *Margaritaville* more times than we could count.

It could be the official theme song of this southernmost point on the continental United States, seemingly playing at every tourist restaurant, bar, and gift shop on this minuscule piece of land 93 miles (150 kilometers) north of Cuba.

I'd driven nearly 1,000 interstate miles (1,600 kilometers) with my photographer buddy, Michael Alan Ross (MAR to his friends, or at least to me), from my home in North Carolina to Key West, Florida, for the start of our epic drive. It would begin at Mile Marker 0 on U.S.-1, then roll across the continental U.S., Canada, and Alaska until we reached the end of the road in Deadhorse, Alaska, some 9,000 miles (11,265 kilometers) north and west from where we started.

Everyone in Key West has a story about Jimmy Buffett, possibly this town's most famous former resident. As we toured the town with my friend Jack Baldwin, he pointed out Buffett landmarks.

"That's the house where he lived before his music career took off," he explained as we stopped in front of a two-story clapboard, a house that had likely been majestic half a century ago. "Now he lives anywhere he wants. He has lots of boats and houses."

Jack also pointed out a small, blocky building near the water, formerly an icehouse before Buffett converted it into a recording studio. "Famous groups still record in that building because it offers a retro sound and the old tube-type equipment everyone seems to be searching for these days."

Buffett will never be a Conch (pronounced "konk"). That's the name given to Key West natives, after the tasty fish caught in the area's waters. Buffett was born in Mississippi and, despite his notoriety and no matter how long he lives in south Florida, he can never be a Conch. Neither can Jack, even though he has lived here for forty-five years.

Newbies like Buffett and Jack will always be thought of as strangers by the locals. Perhaps this humiliation is why Buffett move back to the mainland.

Jack and his wife, Kathryn dePoo, invited us to dinner at the Hogfish Bar & Grill. This traditional Key West seafood restaurant was within walking distance of Boyd's Campground, our home for two nights.

The Sun was beginning to set, but the Key West air remained so thick and humid that we easily broke a sweat during the 1-mile (1.6-kilometer) walk to dinner. En route to Hogfish we were exposed to Key West's grittier underbelly. The ramshackle, unkempt homes one block off Highway 1 offered a sharp contrast to the expensive waterfront homes we'd seen earlier.

As MAR and I approached the restaurant, we noticed that our hosts had already arrived in Jack's beautiful metallic green 1963 Studebaker Avanti. In a funky town better known for its art, music, and food, Jack stands out as one of the island's few car enthusiasts. Restaurant staff and customers left their seats to inspect his stylish ride, which was parked strategically outside the front door. Besides the Avanti, Jack has owned a Chevelle, a Beck Spyder, and a C8 Corvette, and now awaits delivery of a new Z06 Corvette.

During dinner, Kathryn educated us about life in Key West. Kathryn is a true Conch, having been born and raised there, as was her father. Her mother, Suzie Zuzek dePoo, originally from New York, became a renowned Key West artist whose colorful artwork was used for Lilly Pulitzer's women's clothing. Suzie's achievements granted her honorary Conch status.

Kathryn told us about the deterioration of the carefree island lifestyle she'd grown up with. "The billionaires are pushing out the millionaires," she lamented. "I remember when we heard about the first house that sold for $250,000 in the 1970s. We all thought the buyer had been ripped off. What did I know? Now shacks sell for a million dollars."

As we walked back to the campground from dinner, I wondered how many of the rough homes we passed had million-dollar price tags?

Keys Visitor

5 BROTHERS

930 SOUTHARD STREET, KEY WEST, FL 33040

5 Brothers is the real deal when it comes to Cuban coffee. There are lots of places in town who claim to have the best, but this one is it!

MEETING THE LOCALS AT 5 BROTHERS

The next morning MAR was on a mission to find real Cuban-style coffee. On Jack's recommendation, we visited 5 Brothers, a local favorite. The corner store looked like it might have been a candy store a hundred years ago, but at some point it had been converted into one of Key West's most authentic coffee shops. Owner and head barista Pepe Paez brewed up a potent cortado macchiato for MAR, and we joined some of the locals sitting outside eyeing our parked Bronco.

"Where's Deadhorse?"

"When are you leaving?"

"How far is it?"

"I've been waiting six months for a new Bronco. How did you get yours so fast?"

Audrey Samz, one of the locals at 5 Brothers, was holding court on the sidewalk outside the store. She told us we should refer to her as "Supergirl" and further noted that

we should describe her as "a skinny blonde who loves rap music and fast cars."

"I lived in Toronto, but wanted to get away because I had a broken heart," she explained. "So I moved here thirty-two years ago." Supergirl currently owns several cars, "all stick shifts," including a Jeep Wrangler and a BMW M3.

Audrey intended to stay only three months to escape the harsh Canadian winter, but she never left. "Key West is like a community, like a big high school. I lived for a short while in Fort Lauderdale, and I'd go to the same gym and see the same people every day and nobody ever talked. Here people, even strangers, are always inviting me to coffee."

Sitting next to Audrey was John Wilson Smith, a true Conch. John was born and raised in the nearby Bahama Village neighborhood.

Unless you arrive by plane or boat, Highway 1 is the only road you can use to enter or exit the Florida Keys. Built in 1926, well before President Eisenhower's Interstate Highway System of the 1950s, the highway meanders north from its southern terminus in Key West, through fourteen states and the District of Columbia as it hugs the coastline of the eastern states. By the time it reaches Fort Kent, Maine, on the Canadian border, it has covered 2,370 miles (3,815 kilometers), making it the longest north–south road in the United States.

In the Keys, Highway 1 serves as the main road for 120 miles (193 kilometers), connecting this chain of tropical islands via forty-two bridges. Defined as a coral key archipelago, the islands were formed from organic coral deposits. According to the 2020 census, almost 83,000 people live in the Keys, with about 30 percent of those residing in Key West. Thirty of the more than 800 Key islands in the Florida Keys are populated. The furthest keys are 70 miles (113 kilometers) from Key West; these make up Dry

Tortugas National Park. The uninhabited islands are tourist destinations for day trips and camping and can be reached by ferry—but not by Bronco.

The road is populated by numerous sandal outlets, dozens of vendors claiming to be the "Original Key Lime Pie Shop," tourist tchotchke shops, and speed traps where town fathers hope to retain a percentage of tourist dollars to help balance their town's budget and give themselves raises.

Right: This 1940s postcard features one of the 42 Highway 1 bridges that connect the Florida mainland with Key West, 120 miles to the south.(Photo by Print Collector/Getty Images)

"I was 14 and looking for a job, probably walking dogs for the people in the high-rise buildings," he said. "But I discovered greyhound racing and spent forty-five years breeding and training race dogs. I owned sixty to a hundred and twenty at any time and raced them at tracks between here and New Hampshire. I stopped racing dogs five years ago when I was diagnosed with multiple myeloma."

John could never consider any place else home. "There's a portal of love here. People are able to linger. Being Black, I've never been exposed to racism in Key West. We all get along."

Now retired from the greyhound racing business, John meets friends at the coffee shop each morning, then spends his days studying the disappearing local Black history.

"We're writing the last chapter of our history right now."

THE HOME OF KEY LIME PIE

We couldn't leave Key West without sampling a slice of Key lime pie. On Jack's recommendation, we headed to Kermit's Key West Lime Shoppe to try this local culinary delight. The place is immaculate, selling not only Key lime pie but also ice cream, juice, cookies, candy, salsa, and anything else you can imagine that could be made from a lime.

Owner Kermit Carpenter, a local non-Conch celebrity, moved to Key West thirty years ago to open a shop dedicated to the tasty dessert, his version offering the perfect degree of tartness.

A bit of a showman, Kermit wore a chef's uniform and hat and sported a bushy mustache. He walked us through an expertly choreographed sales pitch with the help of a plaster-of-Paris pie as a prop.

Top: Black Gold Coffee owner Gary Lauters (*left*) and fiancée Alyssa Williams, the "Coordinator of Chaos," have built a fun and caring community within their coffee shop. Besides good vibes, the Venice-based shop roasts its own beans, turns out a terrific brew, and offers nice pastries. My cousin Bill, who lives in Alaska, told me he frequents Black Gold whenever he visits his sister Ann in Florida.

Bottom: Kermit Carpenter has taken the local dessert staple, Key lime pie, and turned it into a global brand, offering it in his cafes and retail store, and by mail order. Kermit is as much an actor as he is an entrepreneur, willing to engage in conversation with anybody as he uses his Key lime pie prop in an attempt to bring in more customers.

"When I moved here, Jimmy Buffett used to hide his tour bus next to my building," Kermit told us. He confirmed the recording studio story Jack had told us previously: "The brick building over there was Jimmy's first recording studio. Even today, he and many Nashville stars record there because the sound is unique and it's a cool place to hang out."

Kermit was named after one of President Teddy Roosevelt's seven children, he says. He arrives at his store each morning at 7 a.m. and departs at 4 p.m.—even though the Shoppe stays open until 9:30 p.m. "I've been here seven days a week, 365 days a year, for thirty years."

Key lime pie is made of deceptively simple ingredients: graham cracker crust shell, Key lime juice, egg yolks, and sweetened condensed milk, then topped with whipped cream. The dessert's tartness, and its name, derive from the juice of a specific variety of small lime that grows in year-round warm climates like Florida.

Kermit produces two hundred pies every day from his Key West store. He has another facility 400 miles (644 kilometers) north in Deland, Florida; from there he ships pies, his proprietary ice cream "pie bars," candy bars, sauces, salsas, and numerous other Key lime–related items around the world. Key Lime pie is bittersweet, somehow matching our mood as we wrapped up our too-brief time in Key West and prepared for our very long drive.

AN INAUGURAL SWIM IN THE GULF

We figured we could only spare forty-eight hours to get a handle on life at the nation's southernmost point. After several nice meals, a tour of Papa's Pilar Distillery (offering spirits inspired by Ernest "Papa" Hemingway himself), and a sendoff by Key West Mayor Teri Johnston, we turned our Bronco and Airstream combo north.

But before we hit the road, there was one more task to undertake, part of our road-tripping tradition.

In 2015 MAR and I had retraced Route 66 in my 1939 Ford Woody Wagon. Before leaving Chicago, we filled a water bottle with Lake Michigan water, which we poured ceremonially into the Pacific Ocean upon our arrival in Santa Monica.

In 2017 we'd "baptized" the front tires of a Model T Ford in the Atlantic Ocean before setting off on the Lincoln Highway. At the end of that journey, we immersed the car's rear wheels in the Pacific Ocean.

This history of inaugurating a trip with water led me to a quick swim in the Gulf before we left Key West. I stripped down to my bathing suit within full view of a waterfront bar and took a dip, plunging into water warmer than my morning shower.

Toweling off, I wondered: "Would I have the guts to jump into the freezing Arctic Ocean two months from now?"

FINDING BLACK GOLD IN VENICE

Okay, we cheated in Florida.

Although our plan was to stay off interstate highways all the way from Florida to Alaska, we jumped on I-75 as soon as we exited the Keys. Florida is a huge state, and if we'd stuck to the smaller roads we'd likely still be there. "You can check out any time you like, but you can never leave," as the Eagles song goes.

For the sake of time, we took the fast road up into the mainland, skirted Miami, then took a turn west on what's known as "Alligator Alley" to the Gulf side. We stopped in Venice, north of Fort Myers, where we spent the night at the home of my cousin Ann Keohan and her husband Peter. It would likely be our last home-cooked meal and a night in a real bed for a spell.

"Please, bring me my wine. . . ."

Peter and Ann recommended a great little coffee shop as we said our good-byes the next morning. Black Gold Coffee is 1 mile (1.6 kilometers) from their house, and Ann told me her brother (my cousin), Bill Cotter, makes a point of frequenting Black Gold every time he visits from Alaska.

Walking in, I immediately sensed a nice vibe. The coffee shop buzzed with a pleasant cacophony of conversation and laughter.

Left: Two hours after leaving our Key West campsite, we were thrown back into the harsh reality of rush-hour traffic, interstate highways, and a very long drive to the Georgia state line. We reluctantly decided to take interstates north instead of two-lane roads because Florida is such a long state. If we had taken two-lane roads, we might still be trying to leave!

Above: We finally made it out of Florida! We could have driven directly to Alabama, but to increase our two-lane state count, we crossed into Georgia, if only for a short time.

Right: A highlight of visiting 3 Squares was meeting Cindy, a server there for thirteen years. The grandmother of six made us feel like we were the most important customers in the world, which is what all good restaurant servers used to do. Remember the days when servers would respond to "Thank you" with "You're welcome" instead of "No problem"? Cindy was a wonderful throwback to an earlier era.

We were greeted by Alyssa Williams from behind the counter. She's a vibrant young lady originally from Lubbock, Texas, having come to Venice by way of Washington, D.C. At the start of the coronavirus pandemic, Alyssa packed her things into her Toyota Sienna minivan and hit the road. "I came to Venice because I had family here who I wanted to know and love," she said.

She stumbled into Black Gold Coffee as a customer and never left, eventually becoming an employee and rising to her current role as "Coordinator of Chaos." Better still, Alyssa fell in love with shop owner Gary Lauters, and they're now engaged to be married.

"When Gary and I travel, we visit coffee shops all around the country," she said. "In many of the shops we visit, people don't even talk to each other. Here we have regular customers ranging from eighteen to eighty-three years old, and everyone talks to everyone. One old gentleman can hardly walk, but he comes in every morning to read his newspaper."

Many customers have become close friends. "Last Saturday we were invited to the wedding of two customers, but before we could even leave for the ceremony, two others came into the store to tell us of recent deaths in their families."

"It's all about love and loss before 8 a.m."

BLACK GOLD COFFEE ROASTERS

2385 E. VENICE AVENUE, VENICE, FL 34292

Black Gold has turned its shop into a destination point for the community. Its slogan, "from tree to cup," has caught on with the locals. The lines out the door are solid proof they serve great coffee to happy customers.

CROSSING THE PANHANDLE

We continued our I-75–cheating ways to abet our Florida escape. It felt like we were the only ones heading north: as one of the fastest-growing states in the U.S., Florida sees a lot of vehicles headed one direction—south—with no intention of turning around.

Before jumping on the four-lane highway, though, we stopped at an AutoZone for WD-40—which we hoped would cure a squeaky trailer hitch and preserve our sanity—and an impact socket. When I'd picked up our Airstream Basecamp 16X at the factory in Jackson Center, Ohio, I promised the technician who prepped our trailer that I would torque the new rig's wheels to 115 lb-ft (155 N-m) every 1,000 miles (1,610 kilometers). The standard socket I'd packed was not up to the task and would end up cracking before I got to the fourth wheel lug.

To lose a wheel on our Airstream anywhere on this trip would totally ruin our day.

Florida offers amazing contrasts in scenery. Key West was all beaches and palm trees. Heading north through Miami and Fort Lauderdale, the view was dominated by high-rise buildings and shopping centers. Enough with interstate highways,

already; 500 miles into our trip we abandoned the highway and jumped onto Highway 27 in Alachua. As we continued north, through the Panhandle and approaching the state capital in Tallahassee, we were surrounded by farms, orchards, and large estates. This was clearly the "working" side of the state, more resembling a Midwest farming community than the photos in travel brochures promoting the Sunshine State.

One thing that doesn't change much in Florida is the temperature. As we prepared to leave Ann and Peter's in Venice, the morning temperature had already reached 80°F (27° C)—and it wasn't even 8 a.m.! Reattaching the Airstream to the Bronco had me sweating like a furnace stoker. I hope all those new Florida residents from Wyoming and Colorado are ready for life inside the air-conditioned bubbles that make living there bearable, at least during summer's daylight hours.

By mid-afternoon, 300 miles (483 kilometers) north of Venice, it was a steamy 94°F (34°C) as we rolled in a northeasterly direction through Branford County. North Florida's off-the-beaten-path, small-town main streets look sad with many vacant storefronts. The stores that remained open, like the now light-blue NAPA Auto Parts building we passed, were so faded by the sun that I bet they hadn't been repainted since the Nixon administration.

Above: It was dinnertime and there weren't many places to eat in Donalsonville, Georgia, so we chose the top-rated restaurant in town, 3 Squares Diner. As a frequent traveler, I've learned to seek out family-owned restaurants and avoid franchise chain restaurants whenever possible.
Right: I hadn't visited Dreamland for over twenty years. It's a renowned Birmingham barbecue restaurant with an earthy, authentic vibe, where barbecue is made the old-fashioned way—on a spit over a flame.

FLORIDA SEES A LOT OF VEHICLES HEADED ONE DIRECTION – SOUTH – WITH NO INTENTION OF TURNING AROUND.

By the time we made it to Perry, a town at the point where the Gulf Coast curves into the Panhandle, I was craving a small vanilla cone from a local Dairy Queen, and Perry seemed like the kind of place that might have a DQ.

Sadly I was wrong. We pulled into a Chevron gas station to fuel up the Bronco and I settled for an ice cream sandwich. I imagine that the people who own that station are nice, and the young people behind the counter were certainly friendly, but someone had scrawled an ugly political statement on the wall in the men's room. I wish I hadn't seen it, and I hoped that the discord it suggested would not prove a common thread as we wandered over the next several thousand miles to Alaska.

GEORGIA ON MY MIND

We headed due north from Florida into Georgia boost our trip's "state count," though we only skimmed Georgia as we made the short drive to the Alabama state line. But we stayed long enough for a few adventures and a great meal.

In the town of Brinson, Georgia, I saw a sign, "Home to Maggie Bridges." Who was that? I Googled the name and learned that Maggie had held the title of Miss Georgia while a student at Georgia Tech in 2014. The following year she made the final fifteen in the Miss America pageant. Prior to being Miss Georgia, she was Miss Georgia Fairs (2012), Miss Cobb County (2013), and Miss Capital City (2014).

We didn't have time to stop and meet Maggie, but before we left town I found out more about the town. According to the 2020 U.S. census, Brinson had 216 residents in addition to its one beauty queen—which is not to say the other 216 citizens may not be fetching as well. Like I said, we didn't have time to stop.

Why the rush? We were rolling to dinner in Donalsonville, Georgia, to one of the best places to dine there (according to Tripadvisor)—also, it's the only one. Called the 3 Squares Diner (get it? breakfast, lunch, and dinner), it was ringed by many pickup trucks parked outside, which suggested to us that it had to be good.

MAR and I took seats at a table next to a bunch of older fellows sporting suspenders and John Deere caps and accompanied by their wives who, in their formative years, may or may not have resembled Maggie Bridges from over in Brinson—one never knows. Clearly this was the culinary center of Donalsonville.

Our server, Cindy, seemed positively delighted we'd arrived, like she'd been waiting for us. I asked to see the wine list, but Cindy informed us that they only had Pepsi ("not Coke"), Diet Pepsi, sweet tea, and water. MAR went for the hard stuff—full-strength Pepsi—but I decided to play it safe, opting for the diet version.

"Our most popular item on the menu is the Pork Roast Open Face Sandwich with onions, peppers, and gravy," Cindy enthused. Her excitement was palpable and she spoke with such conviction that I just had to order it. A patty melt or a bowl of chili seemed pointless in light of that glowing recommendation. MAR opted for the grilled-cheese sandwich with bacon.

I asked Cindy why the local downtown was so empty. "I guess people just moved away," she said, noting that she had lived in Donalsonville her entire sixty-five years.

"Yup, born and raised. My mother ran another restaurant up the road for fifty years, and I worked there for thirty."

Today the paper mill is the major industry in Donalsonville, but Cindy said that "you need to be well off or know somebody to work there. Most people around here work at the chicken plant in Dothan, Alabama."

I asked if she was married, to which she firmly replied: "No! I decided a long time ago that I can take care of myself better than someone else can take care of me."

"But I have two sons and six beautiful grandchildren," she bragged, as only a proud grandmother can, "a mixture of White, Filipino, and African American."

Before we left, Cindy gave us each a strawberry short-cake, on the house. As we enjoyed dessert, I asked her how much she liked the Pork Roast Open Faced Sandwich she had talked me into.

"Don't know. Never had it," she winked. "I'm a saleslady, I'll tell you that."

SWEET HOME ALABAMA

As evening fell on our first day in Alabama, we scouted out a KOA campground in Ozark, Alabama, arriving after the office had already closed. But in what seems to be an honor code for campers, we were able to do an after-hours check-in and settle up with management in the morning.

I know KOA is considered the McDonald's of the camping world, but when my wife Pat and I camped out of the back of a Datsun 240Z during the summer of 1978, these campgrounds were our go-to spots to spend the night. Unfailingly they had clean showers and restrooms, neat grounds, and friendly staff. And from what I could tell on our trip to Alaska, not much has changed in the intervening forty years. At $52 a night, including electricity and water, it seems like the best bargain in road-tripping.

South of the Ozark KOA we scoped out a coffee shop we planned on visiting in the morning. Like Jerry Seinfeld,

I'm a bit of a latecomer to the coffee world, having acquired a taste for the beverage only in my early sixties. But MAR is a coffee snob and demands a quality cup of joe before starting his day. Up to this point on the trip, he'd been disappointed. But the next morning, Loose Brick Coffee Company in town fit the bill. Owner Pam Schisler, daughter Elizabeth, and barista Tytona Rogers have a nice little shop in what was once probably a vibrant downtown. Shops like Loose Brick in small towns across the country are helping lead a rebirth of Main Street business. I was optimistic we'd see many more downtown revivals down the road.

BACK IN DREAMLAND

After enjoying our coffee, we sped through rural Alabama for several hours until our stomachs started growling. Lunch was in order. It was noon and we were two hours south of Birmingham, which meant that if we could hang on for a 2 p.m. lunch, we could treat ourselves to some of the best barbecue on the planet.

In a former life, when I was in the auto racing business and NASCAR was running at nearby Talladega, I would often bring clients to an old-school barbecue restaurant in Birmingham. It had been twenty-five years since I'd visited Dreamland, and I hoped it hadn't changed.

I was not disappointed.

The vintage painted-brick building might once have been an auto repair shop or something like it, but now it's home to the best ribs I've ever tasted. Sitting at the edge of the University of Alabama's Birmingham campus, Dreamland is the real deal, attracting patrons of all descriptions. The clientele is a culinary melting pot of humanity, dipped in spicy sauce and served with a side of cornbread.

The food is amazing, offering barbecue sandwiches, plates, and traditional sides like baked beans and coleslaw. If you visit, be warned: grab plenty of napkins because the red sauce will cover the lower half of your happy face. And this food is not kind to those sporting beards or mustaches.

We did our best to comply with Dreamland's formal No Farting ordinance.

GHOST GARAGE

Right: The T-Bird got our attention, but there was so much more. It appeared to be a fifty-year-old scene, frozen in time, with a number of cars and trucks littering the site, while the convenience store and repair shop had collapsed under their own weight. The price of fuel when the car had been parked appeared on the pump at $1.09 for a gallon.

Below: Several Corvairs were scattered around the property—a pickup, a station wagon, and a couple of sedans—but the real gem was hidden in the collapsing garage! I have no idea about its body style or condition. It had been under cover for many years (decades?), so it's probably the pick of the litter.

Driving north on Highway 5, we stumbled across a surreal scene that could have been featured on my YouTube series, *Barn Find Hunter*. In the town of Nauvoo, Alabama, stood a long-shuttered gas station that probably hadn't filled a tank in forty years. Next to the gas pump sat a forlorn 1960 Thunderbird that appeared to have been parked while the owner went inside to buy a pack of Camels but never returned. The car looked to be rusted beyond repair, but it was cool and had a couple of JC Whitney–style custom wheel covers in the back seat, complete with crossed checkered flags on the center cap. Checking a disused pump, we saw the price of gas: $1.09 per gallon. Considering that gas first passed $1.00 a gallon in 1980, this full-size diorama had been created some time ago.

Scattered throughout the overgrown property were more than a dozen other cars, including a couple VW Beetles, a 1969 Mercury Cougar XR, two Lincoln Mark IVs, and four Corvairs. These last included a fairly nice example of a Stepside Corvair 95 pickup truck. The real gem in the collection was an early yellow Corvair peeking out from beneath a pile of rubble in the collapsed garage. I could see only about a 1-foot-square piece of the car, but because it has been out of the weather for at least 40 years, I bet it was in pretty sound condition. Restoration project!

The facts of Muscle Shoals, Alabama, are none too startling. The largest city in Colbert County, it sits along the Tennessee River, and, as of the 2020 U.S. census, it was home to 14,575 citizens. But within those simple facts hides the extraordinary: Muscle Shoals is a musical destination for musicians and rock-and-roll and Blues enthusiasts from around the world.

In the early 1960s, four talented session musicians, known as the Swampers, resigned from the FAME Recording Studios in Muscle Shoals over a dispute and founded the Muscle Shoals Sound Studio in the neighboring town of Sheffield. The building's unique sound qualities, its vintage recording equipment, and the Swampers' musical chops, soon attracted regional, then national, and ultimately international attention.

Muscle Shoals was put on the map when the Rolling Stones recorded their *Sticky Fingers* album in the studio beginning in late 1969. Local residents still remember when the band and its crew stayed in the local Holiday Inn while recording the album. Mick Jagger, Keith Richards, Mick Taylor, Bill Wyman, and Charlie Watts all visited local restaurants for dinner while they were in town.

"They sure didn't dress like us," noted a lifelong resident in a clear understatement.

The Stones opened the floodgates, through which talent poured. Bands and performers who recorded at the now famous studio included such musical royalty as Aretha Franklin, Wilson Pickett, Willie Nelson, Lynyrd Skynyrd, Joe Cocker, Levon Helm, Paul Simon, Bob Seger, Rod Stewart, Cat Stevens, Traffic, Elton John, Boz Scaggs, Bob Dylan, James Brown, and Glenn Frey.

Walking inside, it felt like a holy temple, the walls giving off a sort of humming vibration. Perhaps they were echoes from all the famous acts that had performed there over the decades. The day before we visited, Robert Plant from Led Zeppelin had dropped by!

Who could have imagined that Mick Jagger and Helen Keller both occupied turf only a few miles apart? It's a wonderful world.

Left: It may not look fancy, but back in the day some of the world's top musicians beat a path to the recording studio at Muscle Shoals. Today, musicians and music enthusiasts visit the facility to pay homage to the unique sounds of the building and its talented engineers produced.

Right: One can only imagine the tunes pounded out on this keyboard by everyone from James Brown to Elton John. Now mostly used as a museum, the walls of the place seem to be humming with the sound of bygone legends playing. Hallowed ground.

Bottom: R&B great Wilson Pickett (left) talks with engineer Tom Dowd during a recording session at Muscle Shoals Sound Studio on November 24, 1969. (Photo by Michael Ochs Archives/Getty Images)

A MUSICAL DETOUR

MAR is a car guy: he drives a bitchin' 1951 Shoebox Ford. But he's also a musician who made his living playing guitar in a New Jersey–based rock-and-roll band for twenty-four years. When he realized we were heading toward northwest Alabama, he exclaimed, "We must go to Muscle Shoals!" There was no arguing with him.

I'm someone who loves music, but Muscle Shoals sounded only vaguely familiar. MAR straightened me out.

"For a hot rodder, going to the Bonneville Salt Flats is the ultimate experience," he explained. "For a musician, going to Muscle Shoals is the same thing."

With that we headed due north to the legendary studio. I'd see why it was so special the next morning.

We parked our rig at Heritage Acres RV Park in Tuscumbia, Alabama, an independent campground offering a Deluxe Campsite that included "bathrooms just like the best hotels" for $42 a night. Like our KOA experiences, it was clean, well organized, and managed by a friendly staff. I was getting into this camping stuff.

That night we pulled out all the stops: a main course of peanut butter sandwiches washed down with cans of fine, vintage Dale's Pale Ale.

Ah, the good life.

A VISIT TO HELEN KELLER

Tuscumbia, as it turns out, was the home of Helen Keller. (If that name doesn't ring a bell, watch the movie *The Miracle Worker* with Anne Bancroft and Patty Duke.) We put our quest for Muscle Shoals on hold for the morning so that we could see her birthplace for ourselves.

Helen Keller was born in the Tuscumbia house known as Ivy Green on June 27, 1880. Her early childhood was unremarkable until she contracted a rare illness that left her deaf and blind. When she was seven years old, her doctor, Alexander Graham Bell (yes, the inventor of the telephone) brought twenty-year-old Anne Sullivan into the household to care for Helen and attempt to teach her to communicate.

Helen soon learned the entire alphabet and had learned more than 600 words within six months. By age ten she had mastered Braille and at sixteen could speak well enough to attend school. In 1904 she graduated cum laude from Radcliffe College. She went on to author several books and become a lecturer, mostly on behalf of the American Foundation for the Blind.

MAR and I took the tour of Helen's girlhood home, learned her story, and were smarter in the evening than we had been that morning, a rare occurrence and one of the many benefits of traveling.

Left: It's amazing what we discovered when we got off the beaten path. Our campground was in Tuscumbia, Alabama, the home of Helen Keller. MAR and I took the tour through the house she grew up in and learned about her amazing life from one of the museum's docents.

Right: Meet Maggie the Doberman/flat-coated retriever mix who doesn't like the New Orleans Saints, or so it would appear. We were sitting outside Turbo Coffee in Florence when a man in a Saints cap tried to fist-bump Kris, Maggie's owner. Maggie charged the man in a split second, spilling coffee everywhere and scaring the hell out of the guy.

NOT MY FIRST RODEO

This diagonal route across the United States marks the fifth time I've driven from the East Coast to the West Coast along one path or another. At least two of those earlier jaunts were roundtrip. My first coast-to-coast trip was in summer 1978. My wife Pat had the summer off from teaching, and I was between jobs. I'd decided that owning a foreign car repair shop, Sunshine Garage, was not all it was cracked up to be. Long hours, low pay, and constantly dirty hands made me crave a career change. I gave my share of the business to my partner, John McDonald, and committed to work in a Manhattan furniture store that my friend Bill Etts was opening in the fall.

Pat and I left home in our 1971 Datsun 240Z and took a 9,000-mile (14,500-kilometer) lap around the United States over the course of six weeks. I'd purchased the Z for $900 several months before the trip. It had a blown head gasket and needed bodywork, but by the time we left Long Island, that overhead-cam six-cylinder purred like a kitten. I could hit 100 miles per hour (161 kilometers per hour) in third gear, no problem.

We wanted to escape the New York metropolitan area as quickly as possible, so we left our rental house in St. James, on Long Island, at 4 a.m. and drove virtually non-stop until nightfall when we reached South Bend, Indiana, almost 1,000 miles (1,609 kilometers) away.

I was so naive. I'd never been that far west before. We were driving on I-80, entering Ohio from Pennsylvania, when we saw a highway sign: "Ohio, Gateway to the Midwest!"

"Babe, we're almost there," I told Pat, imagining I could already smell the Pacific Ocean breezes. Then I realized we were actually still 2,000 miles (3,219 kilometers) from the West Coast.

The Datsun ran fine, though hot, and we both made it back to New York in plenty of time to begin our jobs in the fall.

My second cross-country drive was with my friend Peter Egan, then editor at *Road & Track* magazine. Together we drove my recently purchased AC Cobra from the San Francisco Bay Area to my home in North Carolina. We stayed off interstate highways and were in no hurry, so we stretched it out to a nine-day adventure: a trip of a lifetime.

If you've ever watched my YouTube program, *Barn Find Hunter*, you might remember seeing my automotive costar, a 1939 Ford Deluxe Woody Station Wagon. What you may not know is that I bought that car for $300 in 1969 when I was just fifteen years old. My hope was to emulate the life of "typical" California teenagers, who at the time all appeared to surf, drive hot rods, and have amazing blonde girlfriends. My dream was to drive the woody across the United States on a surfing safari when I was old enough to get a driver's

license. It didn't happen for lots of reasons: no money, lack of mechanical skills, school, work, and so on.

Three decades later, after I'd installed a modern drivetrain, my son Brian and I finally took that cross-country surfing safari in the woody between his sophomore and junior year in high school. This was my third time across the country, during which I introduced Brian to some of my friends on the coast, like Tommy Ivo, Dean Jeffries, Keith Martin, and others. Sadly we never got around to actually surfing.

For my next major cross-country run, MAR, our friend Brian Barr, and I drove my woody from Chicago to L.A. on Route 66 for my book, *Route 66 Barn Find Road Trip*. A video team from Hagerty also tagged along for a few days to shoot a demo for what would become *Barn Find Hunter*, which opened a new career for me.

My most recent cross-country run was the most epic. For my book *Ford Model T Coast-to-Coast*, MAR (who drove our support Ford Fusion), my friend Dave Coleman, and I drove a 1926 Model T Ford. We started at 42nd Street and Broadway in New York City, kept going all the way on the Lincoln Highway (through thirteen states), and ended up at the Golden Gate Bridge. It was an amazing trip and, believe it or not, completely trouble free on the Model T front.

I guess it was inevitable that I would hatch another road trip scheme. Deadhorse here I come.

"FOR A HOT RODDER, GOING TO THE BONNEVILLE SALT FLATS IS THE ULTIMATE EXPERIENCE," MAR EXPLAINED. "FOR A MUSICIAN, GOING TO MUSCLE SHOALS IS THE SAME THING."

TURBO COFFEE

312 EAST TENNESSEE STREET, FLORENCE, AL 35630

Turbo Coffee is a must when visiting Muscle Shoals. You can't go wrong with their great cortado and a fresh doughnut.

BEWARE OF DOG

When the going gets boring, the bored get coffee. Since the Muscle Shoals Museum didn't open until 10 a.m., we had time to look for the perfect place for our morning java. The best online reviews brought us to Turbo Coffee just over the Tennessee River in Florence, Alabama.

I ordered my usual manly beverage: iced latte with oat milk, heavy on the ice and with an extra espresso shot. Since we'd left Key West, MAR had consistently ordered the same caffeinated drink, a cortado, only to be disappointed time and again when the barista admitted they'd never heard of such a drink. When MAR asked for a cortado at Turbo Coffee, the barista said. "No problem."

"You mean you know what that is?" asked an ecstatic MAR. "Sure do," she answered.

As we sat outside awaiting our drinks, we chatted with a woman who had a large black dog lying at her feet. She introduced her dog, Maggie, before she introduced herself. Kris had moved to nearby Sheffield, Alabama, only a week before.

"Actually, her formal name is Magnolia," Kris said of her dog, "and she is very protective of me." Insert minor chords of foreshadowing here.

"I adopted her in October 2018. I had a DNA test done to determine her breed. It came back dachshund, which is obviously not the case."

Kris told us the tests proved Maggie also had traces of golden retriever, Doberman pinscher, and flat-coated retriever. I'd never heard of a flat-coated retriever, so she explained that they're known as the Peter Pan of dogs: "They never grow up."

As we chatted, a young couple walked past the store holding hands. The man was wearing a New Orleans Saints cap. Kris, who had been living in the Big Easy until the week before, said, "Go Saints," as they walked by. The man stuck out his hand for a harmless fist bump and Maggie, who apparently read it as a potential attack, charged him, flipping the table and chair, and spilling Kris' coffee onto the sidewalk. Kris managed to restrain Maggie, and the startled man and his girlfriend escaped unharmed.

"I told you she was protective."

So much for Peter Pan.

THE DOLLAR GENERAL

What was the store we'd seen the most frequently on our route thus far? McDonald's? Wrong. Shell gas stations? Nope. Dairy Queen? Not by a long shot.

It was Dollar General. That distinctive black-and-yellow sign had haunted us on the road since we'd left Key West. It makes me wish we'd started counting them from the beginning, but who knew?

As of October 2022, 18,634 Dollar General stores operate in the Continental United States. I suspect if we were driving along interstate highways, we wouldn't have seen as many. On our rural two-lane route, though, the stores were everywhere, from small, nearly out-of-business towns to medium-sized cities. They lurked in the outskirts even on rural two-lane roads surrounded by farmland with no houses in sight.

On one stretch of highway there were two Dollar General stores 1½ miles (2.4 kilometers) apart on the same road. What? It turns out that company research has determined people don't want to travel more than thirty minutes to a grocery store, so Dollar General's philosophy is to open "corner grocery stores on steroids," in areas often overlooked by competitors.

MISSISSIPPI FOR A MINUTE

Heading west after our Muscle Shoals tour, we quickly crossed into Mississippi and celebrated by stopping at a Baskin-Robbins ice cream store. We both ordered a Jamoca Almond Fudge cone. Our ice cream almost lasted the short distance it took to cross the state line into Tennessee.

Mississippi was the first instance of visiting a state simply for the sake passing through. This was not by design: I'd simply drawn a diagonal line on a map of the United States, from Florida to Seattle, establishing a very rough route for our journey. That meant we would cut across the corners of several states as we rolled along.

Alabama, Mississippi, Tennessee, Arkansas—we'd pass through each and drive on within a few hours.

That reality acknowledged, we often inadvertently encountered interesting sites. For example, while two-laning near Brownsville, Tennessee, we found ourselves on the 42-mile-long (68-kilometer-long) "Tina Turner Highway," AKA Tennessee Highway 19.

WHAT MAKES DRIVING INTO THE APPROACHING HAVOC SO SCARY IS THE UNKNOWN: COULD A TORNADO BE BREWING OUT THERE? SHOULD WE SEEK COVER?

Tina Turner. Yes, that Tina Turner, the "Queen of Rock." Born Anna Mae Bullock in Brownsville in 1939, the future Tina Turner lived in nearby Nutbush during her formative years, where she attended the Nutbush Elementary School, then George Washington Carver High School.

Anna Mae, then Little Ann, and finally Tina in 1960, eventually moved to St. Louis, where she met Ike Turner, and the rest is history—though not always a happy story.

Still her career skyrocketed both as a member of Ike & Tina Turner, and during her solo career. Not bad for a cheerleader and basketball player from Tennessee.

THROUGH A STORM, ALMOST TO INDIANAPOLIS

Okay, Tennessee isn't a Gulf state like the others in this chapter. And it's not in the Midwest either. But it is *adjacent* to the Gulf states of Mississippi and Alabama, so. . .

In any case, we had bigger concerns than regionality. We were not quite 20 miles (32 kilometers) from the Mississippi River, driving northbound in Tennessee toward Dyersburg, and a major storm loomed ahead. You know the type: an angry sky building far in the distance, layers of light and dark gray clouds rolling in the direction you're driving.

The flashes of lightning begin, followed quickly by thunder. Then the largest raindrops known to man slap your windshield and the sky opens up.

As we headed into the brooding dark, the temperature dropped from 88° to 62°F (31° to 17°C) in a mere fifteen minutes.

What makes driving into the approaching havoc so scary is the unknown: could a tornado be brewing out there? Should we seek cover? Find an overpass to park under?

MAR was at the wheel, ready to face down what lay ahead, but we had to stop eventually. Setting up camp in the pouring rain was not our first choice, so we watched for a hotel. Thankfully the storm passed, along with considering a hotel. We cruised toward the Mississippi River following a westward path and into clear weather.

We actually considered making a banzai side trip to Indiana for Indianapolis 500 qualifying weekend. After a yes-no-yes-no-yes session, we let the clock and GPS make the call.

Qualifying for positions one through twelve was to begin at 4 p.m. and it was already 11:30 a.m. GPS told us we'd arrive in Speedway, Indiana, at 4:35 p.m., late for the beginning of qualifying, but in time for the next session for positions one through six, which would begin at 5:10 p.m.

What to do? If we didn't need to stop for fuel or nature, we *might* make it thirty minutes late, but more likely it would be a major effort for a small window of track time. "What do you think?" I asked MAR.

"It seems forced," he sighed, even though he'd never been to Indianapolis Motor Speedway and really wanted to go.

I got it. He was absolutely correct.

I hadn't been to Indy, or the 500, since 1994, when my then-client Mercedes-Benz supplied engines for the Roger Penske cars of Al Unser Jr., Emerson Fittipaldi, and Paul Tracy (who qualified 1st, 3rd, and 25th respectively). Little Al walked away with the win that year. He told me after the race that the Mercedes-Benz/Ilmor engine had so much power—in excess of 1,000 horsepower—that he could spin the back wheels in top gear going down the front straight.

It was an amazing win, and the opportunity to stand on the Bricks with Roger and Al was a dream come true, but my return engagement to the Brickyard was not going to happen this time.

Below: The sky was darkening and we hoped to find a campsite ahead of the rain. Thankfully it was a brief but intense shower. We set up camp at the storm's conclusion.

2.
DEFINITELY
MIDWEST

MISSOURI WALTZ

In the southeastern corner of Missouri, in the town of Fredericktown, we went shopping at a Walmart store for provisions, cleaning supplies, and whatnot.

We decided early on that we would buy items only when they were needed. As an example, I've heard of many people who, before hiking the Appalachian Trail, spend huge amounts of money on equipment—tent, sleeping bag, cooking gear, and other equipment. Within a week or two of starting their five-month walk, which extends from Georgia to Maine, they have sold, given away, or discarded much of their newly purchased equipment because it was either too heavy, unnecessary, or not suitable for the climate.

For our Bronco-Airstream trip, we vowed we'd buy as we went. At the Fredericktown Walmart we bought granola, yogurt (we were trying to eat healthy), beer (all those healthy grains and hops), peanut butter, jelly, Dave's Killer Bread, and a toaster.

For decades I've had ideological issues with Walmart. The stores often set up for business on the outskirts of town and subsequently put the old downtown out of business. I decided to test that belief after we stocked up (perhaps proving my theory in advance). From Walmart, we followed signs to Historic Fredericktown Downtown. As I suspected, it was rather depressing, with eighteen occupied storefronts and sixteen vacant. The occupied stores included a nail salon, a hair salon, barber shop, tax service, insurance office, secondhand stores, and similar small shops. There were no stores selling groceries, and it didn't appear that any store recently in business would have sold food items. I'm sure there must have been a grocer at some point, but the contrast between that low-energy downtown and the bright, shiny Walmart, with its huge variety of fresh meats, fruits, and often local vegetables (even organics) was striking. I'm willing to bet no store in Fredrickson's downtown past ever offered that kind of selection.

Although I never thought I would admit this, at least in some communities, I think Walmart has actually improved the lives, diets, and health of people who shop there.

SAME NAME, DIFFERENT STATE

Happy coincidence! My son Brian and his girlfriend, Camila, had driven up from Atlanta to Springfield, Illinois, for the wedding of his former college roommate. I looked on the map and saw that we were east of Springfield.

"Hey, Brian, we're only a couple of hours apart. We should meet for breakfast," I texted him. I had seen Brian a number of times over the past couple of months, but had not seen Camila. It would be great to see them.

We made plans the night before: we'd both leave at 8 a.m., I would drive west and they would drive east, and we'd meet somewhere in the middle. We sorted it by text:

Tom: Let's just both get on Highway 60.

Brian: That's three hours south of me. I'm on Route 66 near St. Louis.

Tom: Can't be. I'm looking at the map right now.

Brian: Something's not right. Dad, are you talking about Springfield, Illinois?

That's when I found out there's more than one Springfield in the Midwest.

Camila called my cell phone: "Dad, there is a Springfield in *every* state in the country."

Darn, I thought they were in Springfield, Missouri. The planned meetup was a bust.

For the record, not *every* state has a Springfield, just thirty-four states. Still, on road trips as in life, it's helpful to be 100% certain you know where you are.

Right: What meal could be more appropriate for America's Greatest Road Trip than a good old PB and J? It's the most versatile meal on the planet and requires no talent to produce this simple, nutritious sandwich—suitable for breakfast, lunch, or dinner!

THE COFFEE ETHIC

124 PARK CENTRAL SQUARE, SPRINGFIELD, MO 65806

Coffee Ethic is a *must* when traveling Route 66. It was so good we had to visit twice. What a great surprise to have your cortado delivered with a sparkling water chaser without having to ask.

Left: "Hey, I know you!" Chad and Jenny Mitchell, from British Columbia, are fans of my *Barn Find Hunter* program on YouTube. They were on a multiweek motorcycle adventure that would take them from Myrtle Beach, South Carolina, to Arizona, before they turned north and headed back to their four children in B.C.
Right: The devil made me do it. I saw this small paved road crossing a stream as MAR drove along. "Turn around!" I shouted. We spent twenty minutes there, traversing the stream, back and forth, trying to capture the ideal "splash" photo. This is it!

ZEN LUNCH

The next morning we woke to an air temperature of 52°F (11°C), the coldest we'd experienced up to that point. I packed away my shorts and T-shirt and pulled out jeans and a sweatshirt.

We'd planned to stay on two-lane roads all the way across America, but sometimes your plans don't match up with reality. Often those two-lane roads are best accessed by a connecting jaunt on a four-laner.

Missouri treated us well in this regard: we found a couple of rural routes—Highways 72 and 32—that were two-lane dreams. They were smooth, sweeping, and occasionally challenging, bordered by beautiful farm fields and homesteads. This was the two-lane America I had in my mind.

We stopped for lunch at a roadside picnic site with the unusual name of Daisaku Ikeda Tip-Top Roadside Park, a little pull-off on an elevated portion of roadway with a couple of picnic tables and a pleasant view of the countryside. It is named for a Japanese Buddhist philosopher, author, and poet laureate who wrote stories and poems of serenity. The folks who established the park hoped visitors would be inspired by Ikeda's philosophy. A plaque on a rock offered an excerpt from his book *The Human Revolution*:

People can only live fully
By helping others live.
When you give life to friends
You truly live.
Cultures can only realize
Further richness
By honoring other traditions.
And only by respecting natural life
Can humanity continue to exist.

We contemplated this wisdom as we enjoyed our peanut butter and jelly sandwiches.

CANADIAN CRUISERS

"Hey, I know you!"

We had checked into a very nice KOA in Springfield, Missouri (not Illinois), and were headed to the laundry room to take care of a week's worth of road-worn clothes, when a guy standing next to his Harley-Davidson called to me.

"You're that Barn Find guy!"

He introduced himself as Chad Mitchell. His wife, Jenny, accompanied him on another Harley.

Chad rode a 2021 Street Glide Special, and Jenny a 2014 Low Rider.

The couple from British Columbia looked to have more packed onto their two bikes than we had in our Bronco *and* Airstream: tent, sleeping bags, weather gear, party lights (really!), a bottle of Jack Daniels, a French press coffeemaker (really!), cooking utensils, probably a collapsible hot tub (not really). They had a huge campfire roaring next to their tent.

"We left the four kids with my mom, and we've been on the road for two-and-a-half weeks already," said Jenny. "We attended the wedding of a relative in Durham, North Carolina, and Bike Week at Myrtle Beach, South Carolina. From here we're heading toward Moab, up through Arizona, trying to stay toward the south for the nice weather."

Chad showed us photos of the 1936 Plymouth coupe street rod he was building. He had taught himself sheet-metal fabrication and rebuilt his own floors and transmission tunnel.

"Jen is supposed to be back at work as a paramedic next Sunday, but that's not going to happen," said Chad. "She'll need to call in sick, because we won't be home for about ten days."

I thought, maybe we'll see them again when we pass through British Columbia in a few weeks' time.

MINI-BOOMTOWN

Springfield, Missouri, is a great little city. So much so that we decided to spend another day there. I mean, there were *eleven* coffee shops in town for MAR to sample!

What makes a small city like Springfield hip when so many others we'd passed through were virtually vacant? I'm not naive or arrogant: I know that once-thriving small towns in the middle of farm country may be on a downturn for any number of reasons.

Agriculture is not the main industry in Springfield. The town is home to four college campuses, including Missouri State University, and the corporate headquarters for Bass Pro Shops and Andy's Frozen Custard are located here. Old commercial buildings are being converted to residential lofts and stylish new businesses, making Springfield a popular regional destination.

And beer. I'm a true believer that craft breweries can help revitalize a depressed downtown, and Springfield has thirteen breweries, as well as several distilleries and wineries. Drink up, weary traveler!

A WINDING ROAD IN THE RAIN

We rounded out our first week on the road with two days in Springfield. Having enjoyed our extended visit, it was time to get back on the road. The weather was cool, and the forecast called for rain beginning in the midmorning and continuing for the next couple of days.

I'd received recommendations for a circuitous two-lane route heading west from Springfield into Kansas from my friends in Kansas City, Penny Sharp and Jim Sfetko. We took their advice and were soon on a twisty road surrounded by pleasant scenery. No regrets, though the pouring rain didn't put us in the mood to stop for sightseeing.

Many modern roads are generic and flat, with much of the natural topography bulldozed flat to make them safer. True country roads, though, often follow the paths of ancient trails or property boundaries. At the very least, they traverse the natural terrain with all the on-and-off-camber turns and elevation changes that remain millions of years after the great glaciers retreated.

The route that morning was familiar: we were on a road we'd driven eight years before while working on another book, *Route 66 Barn Find Road Trip*. For that adventure, we drove the length of the Mother Road from Chicago to Santa Monica, all the while searching for neglected and forgotten old cars. As we cruised along this time, we remembered an exact car, or barn, or junkyard from our 2014 junket. Change happens more slowly here on the prairie.

KANSAS CALM

We drove a couple of arrow-straight and lonely two-lane roads across eastern Kansas to McPherson, a prairie town I know well. It's almost in the middle of the state, about three hours west of Kansas City and an hour north of Wichita.

I become instantly calm whenever I reach this part of the country. Folks who live out here seem more at peace with their lives than those of us on the coasts. It would probably be a healthy lifestyle change if I decided to move here, the middle of the country.

SUPER 2

After coffee and breakfast at Craft Coffee in downtown McPherson, we drove thirty minutes north to Salina for lunch with my friends Roger and Sissy Morrison, along with Roger's brother Richard.

Roger is one of the most enthusiastic car guys I've ever met. He owns 100-year-old Rolls-Royces, Porsches, a couple of Mercedes-AMG station wagons, hot rods, a woody, three Shelby GT350s, and an AC Cobra. Whenever I'm in this part of the country, a visit with Roger and Sissy is always in order.

Before MAR and I departed Salina, Roger and Richard gave us a list of suggested two-lane roads leading west and north toward Nebraska: Highway 14 North, Highway 24 West, Highway 181 North, then Highway 281 North to the Nebraska state line.

Before we hit the road again, we wanted to get an air bag warning light on the Bronco checked. A visit to Long McArthur Ford in Salina quickly addressed the issue. This family-owned dealership dates back to 1950, and we appreciated the friendly, competent staff. As often happens with modern cars, the warning light was a nonissue and only needed to be cleared up with a simple computer fix. A big thank-you to Long McArthur for the speedy pit stop.

The Morrisons' route took us through the beautiful heart of Kansas, its small towns and rich farmland, past grain silos and oil derricks. Richard's route gave me a new road description to ponder. Even though all the highways would be two lanes, he said some might be "Super 2s."

"A Super 2?" I asked Richard.

"It's a higher-speed two-lane with wide shoulders for quick travel."

Here I am, thinking of myself as the ultimate road warrior, but I'd never heard of a Super 2. *Continued on page 45*

This college sits in the middle of you-can't-get-there-from-here America. I should know—I travel there at least once each year fulfilling my duties as a member of the college's National Advisory Board for Automotive Restoration.

And now a few words about my favorite post-secondary educational institution.

McPherson College offers the nation's only four-year Bachelor of Science in Automotive Restoration Technology. We in the collector-car world worry constantly about what will happen with our collections and our hobby when we're gone. Who will take up the torch? Who will maintain, repair, and love our old crocks? McPherson College provides an answer. Its automotive restoration program is part of the college's School of Business. Students take classes in math, history, and science, as in any liberal arts college, but they also study metal fabrication, engine building, upholstery, and auto body and paint.

I asked Brian Martin, senior director of auto restoration, to explain the unique program:

The difference between an auto tech school and McPherson is the academic and liberal arts education we bring to a student's education. We don't teach for a job, but for a career, by exposing students to the science of how a car works, the history of the automobile, and the chemistry of paint and the art of color. Many students arrive as freshmen with the idea of going into street rods after graduation, but after four years they fall in love with brass era cars and decide to go in that direction.

McPherson launched the program in 1976. Of the small school's over 700 students, about 150 are enrolled in the auto restoration program, with forty-five to fifty new students arriving each year.

Auto restoration students fall into two categories: traditional or nontraditional. Twenty-two-year-old Jackie Gullion comes from Fremont, California. She's a traditional student: though Jackie always liked cars—especially rat rods—she didn't see herself as college material when she was in high school. Then she learned of the auto restoration program from her father, who'd met a couple McPherson students at a Pebble Beach Concours d'Elegance event.

"But I'm so glad I came," says Jackie, a 2022 grad. "It gave me direction."

She didn't have a special focus of study until she interned at Motion Products, a premier Ferrari restoration facility located in Wisconsin, during her junior semester. "I was there working on upholstery and asked if I could try working with metal and aluminum, and they said yes."

That experience helped Jackie discover her life's work. Motion Products offered Jackie a job upon graduation, and she accepted. When we visited, she was assembling her 1967 Mercury Cougar project car, readying it to be towed to her new home in the Cheese State.

"When I started at McPherson four years ago, I never thought I'd be going to work on Ferrari bodies," said Jackie, who's also preparing to publish her second self-published book of poetry. "Coming here helped me break out of my shell."

Nontraditional students are usually older. They may have had another career in a completely unrelated field. Currently, McPherson has several nontraditional students in the program, including a former NFL player.

Ben Wiebe is twenty-nine years old. Hailing from Scotts Bluff, Nebraska, he's a nontraditional student, having formerly managed a hydroponic research facility, a high-stress job that combines water and electricity.

"I was buying, fixing, and selling old VWs and 4X4 Toyotas on the side with my dad," he explained. "When Covid-19 came on, I started weighing my priorities. I thought, if I could bring my management skills to the old car industry, it could provide my wife and me a more pleasant lifestyle and allow us to build a family."

We spoke with Ben at his other job, a barista at Craft Coffee in McPherson.

Bonus: Ben made a killer cortado that even impressed the demanding MAR!

On a cold and rainy Kansas night, the McPherson folks took pity on MAR and me, offering lodging in the recently vacated Morrison Hall dormitory. It was a throwback experience using communal bathrooms and showers, but a pleasant break from the cramped Airstream.

Top: McPherson College is home to perhaps the most respectable auto restoration facility on the planet. Not only does the school turn out beautiful restorations, it teaches students the correct methods to restore vintage vehicles through its four-year bachelor of arts program in that field.
Bottom: Brian Martin, a graduate of the McPherson Auto Restoration program, now serves as its program director and works alongside a half-dozen professors and the 150 students who hope to make a career in the collector car industry, whether in restoration, curation, collection management, journalism, history, or education.

Top: This 1956 Mercedes-Benz 300S Cabriolet is McPherson College's most ambitious auto restoration project to date. For six years, students have been involved in the Concours project, with the hope of displaying the completed car at the 2023 Pebble Beach Concours d'Elegance.

Bottom: Jacqueline Gullion enrolled at McPherson reluctantly after her father heard about the auto restoration program. During her freshman year, she was most interested in rat rods, but over the course of four years she changed her focus to metal fabrication. Upon graduation, Jackie was recruited by a top Ferrari restoration shop to fabricate body panels.

STRUNG-OUT

How could we pass through Cawker City and not visit one of the most celebrated tourist landmarks of all time? You've undoubtedly heard of it, and you may know someone who's been lucky enough to visit Cawker City, Kansas. But for you, dear reader, and for the good of all mankind, we decided we see it for ourselves: the World's Largest Ball of Twine!

And there it was for all the world to see, free of charge, sheltered by its own little gazebo in the middle of town, all 27,017 pounds (12,255 kilograms) of it. An astonishing 46 feet (14 meters) in circumference, the ball is made of 8,507,430 feet (2,593,060 meters) of twine. That's 1,611 miles (2,593 kilometers)—over half the distance from New York City to the West Coast.

Before he died in 1974, creator Frank Stoeber used 1.6 million feet (486,650 meters) of twine collected from years of tying hay bales to fabricate a ball of twine 11 feet (3.4 meters) in diameter. Not wanting to see Stoeber's work become yesterday's news, fellow Cawker City residents occasionally got together in a sort of twine-a-thon, helping increase the ball to a circumference of more than 40 feet (12.2 meters) by 2006. And the city claims it's still growing!

Over the years, there have been numerous claims as to which city has the largest ball of twine. The largest created by a single person resides in Darwin, Minnesota. Francis Johnson began rolling twine in March 1950, and continued for four hours each day for twenty-nine years. Before she passed,

Right: When a dashboard warning light flashed a signal about our Bronco's airbag, we visited Long McArthur Ford in Salina. Our vehicle, and our adventure, intrigued the service technicians and management, who set to work remedying the issue ASAP.

BRONCO REDUX

I own and have owned numerous unusual cars—Cobras, woodies, 4-speed 428 Ford Country Squires, and so on—but this Bronco gets more attention than any car I've ever driven. In any parking lot, folks rush over to ask how I like it, how I managed to get one so soon, and—would I sell it?

The Bronco was the tow vehicle I wanted for this trip because it represented a modern, second-gen version of an iconic SUV. In fact, the term SUV hadn't even been invented when the original Bronco debuted in 1966. Ford's new Bronco offered a 2.0 version that would nicely match the 2.0 version of the trailer I had in mind, the Airstream Basecamp.

I called my friends at Ford Motor Company, who in the past have loaned MAR and me several vehicles for past book projects, and prevailed on them once again. I was rebuffed initially because (1) Broncos were selling themselves, and Ford didn't need additional promotion when their order books were already full, and (2) there were simply no press vehicles to be had. The amazing Diane Southall, who always seems to solve my vehicle issues, came to the rescue, finding a press vehicle that already had lots of miles on it and was about to head to auction.

I picked up the Bronco in Dearborn, Michigan, about two months before the trip, and used it a bit to get familiar with its operation. Knowing my plans for the vehicle, Ford engineers equipped it with an elec-

tric trailer-braking system, a roof rack, and an extra spare tire for that long, potentially treacherous haul up and back on the Dalton Highway to Deadhorse.

By the time we were in Kansas, I'd driven the Bronco more than 4,000 miles (6,437 kilometers), and I was sold on this twenty-first century version. When we finally return it to Ford, I'll likely have rolled some 10,000 miles (16,090 kilometers) in it. It's an ideal vehicle for a sporty individual or family. Ford did their homework and dialed in just enough of the vintage Bronco to be authentic, but with modern technology to make it a relevant and viable alternative in the current car market.

I'd be proud to park one in my garage for the long term—assuming I could lay hands on another.

World's Largest
Ball of Sisal Twine
Started by Frank Stoeber in 1953

8,507,430 FEET   27,017 POUNDS

Left: This sign at the World's Largest Ball of Twine in Cawker City, Kansas, tells it all. One can only imagine how many travelers have shifted their vacation routes to visit the tiny town and see this (un)natural wonder.

Below: I'd heard about the World's Largest Ball of Twine for decades, but never thought it actually existed. But there we were, facing one of the oddest, yet most compelling tourist attractions in the United States.

FOR YOU, DEAR READER, AND FOR THE GOOD OF ALL MANKIND, WE DECIDED TO SEE IT FOR OURSELVES: THE WORLD'S LARGEST BALL OF TWINE!

the ball had grown to 12 feet (3.7 meters) in diameter and weighed 17,400 pounds (7,893 kilograms).

Now that I've seen Cawker City's ball of twine, I'm on a mission to visit some of the world's other great attractions: the Great Pyramids, Stonehenge, and the World's Largest Cheeto (check it out in Algona, Iowa).

BARNYARD PERFUME IN NEBRASKA

We crossed the Kansas-Nebraska state line on Highway 281 North at about 7 p.m. on a windy, cloudy Wednesday evening, passing through the colorful towns of Red Cloud and Blue Hill.

Immediately on the Nebraska side, we spotted a parking area with some informational display boards about the surrounding prairies—appropriate since we were surrounded on all sides by vast fields and grazing cows. As I got out of the Bronco to read them, I immediately smelled agriculture. Not a nasty smell, mind you, but one that reminded me we were a long way from Key West.

The next sense I experienced was sound. The cows on the nearby hills mooed as I walked across the parking lot, as if to say, "Hello, stranger! Welcome to Nebraska!"

Nebraska's plains appear endless. Looking toward the horizon must have been as awe inspiring for the early settlers as it was for me.

Our path from this point would diverge from the Sharpie-traced diagonal route I'd drawn when we planned our trip. We would now go due north through Nebraska, South Dakota,

and North Dakota. Why the route change? Simple: neither of us had ever been to North Dakota. For me it would be the fiftieth state I'd visited. And for MAR, closing in on fifty states himself, it would leave him with only Louisiana and Alaska to visit.

AN ODYSSEY IN HASTINGS

The Sun was sinking and we still had an hour's drive to reach our campground near Grand Island, Nebraska.

If we waited any later to eat dinner, our only choice would likely be gas station hot dogs from Casey's General Store. Not that there's anything wrong with that, but I prefer a balanced meal when possible.

"Michael, there's a city ahead, Hastings," I said. "Maybe we can grab a quick dinner there before it gets too late."

As we drove along Hastings' main drag, a hot rod Cadillac CTS pulled alongside us at a traffic light. The driver motioned that he wanted to talk with us. We rolled down the window.

"How many miles have you traveled so far?" The Bronco's graphics were intended to initiate conversations just like this one.

We told him about 2,500 (4,023 kilometers).

"And you're going all the way to Alaska?"

"Yup, it's over 7,000 miles."

"You guys must be looking for a place to eat," he guessed. "We have one really good restaurant in town, Odyssey. You should eat there, then come over to Tank for a beer. It's kind of a dive bar."

Right: Reaching Nebraska meant we had had only five more states to get through before crossing into Canada. My one visit to the Cornhusker State before had been during a cross-country trip for a previous book, *Ford Model T Coast to Coast*. I truly love visiting here.

Taking his suggestion, we parked our rig and walked over to Odyssey. What a surprise! It was truly special, not the kind of restaurant I expected at all. It was a five-star experience in our book. Great vibe, atmosphere, decor, bar, and staff. Like the rest of Hastings' downtown, the restaurant occupied one of the city's older buildings. The designer had kept enough of its old brick and fixtures that, when combined with modern elements, gave it the feel of a trendy coastal eatery, not a typical Midwestern establishment. The food was spectacular—truly gourmet. The manager explained that the owner had two successful restaurants in town, one a little noisier than this one, for families, and Odyssey, which was more for special occasions.

AN OLD FRIEND: THE LINCOLN HIGHWAY

We woke up in our campsite outside the town of Doniphan, south of the Platte River from Grand Island. It was 50°F (10°C) and sunny, with the stiff wind you expect on the wide-open prairie, where no mountains, trees, or buildings impede it.

Most mornings we made our own breakfast: yogurt with granola for MAR, avocado toast for me. No different today. On this day, we packed up and decided to find a coffee shop in Grand Island, taking the long way into town. We wanted to travel on Highway 30—the Lincoln Highway—for at least a short distance.

It was a flashback to a road trip of yesteryear: A few years before, MAR had followed our friend Dave Coleman and me as we drove every inch of that highway in a Model T Ford—from Times Square in New York City clear to San Francisco's Golden Gate Bridge. The result trip was recorded in the book *Ford Model T Coast-to-Coast*. If you're hungry for even more road-tripping adventures, look for a copy.

INTO THE SAND HILLS

I started this journey—and this book—with the goal of discovering forgotten two-lane America, visiting the towns, seeing the sights, and meeting the people who are often overlooked by travelers blurring across the country on the Interstate Highway System.

I checked our road map and saw the faint line of a road called Nebraska Highway 2. It ran diagonally northwest from Grand Island to the upper corner of Nebraska near the South Dakota state line.

As it turned out, Highway 2 was a gem of a road. Richard Morrison would probably consider it a Super 2, with its wide shoulders and posted speed limit of 65 miles per hour (105 kilometers per hour), higher than other two-lane routes throughout the state.

It took us through the Nebraska Sand Hills, which make up much of the north-central part of the state, roughly 19,300 square miles (5,000 square kilometers). The dunes are a result of sediment washed down from the Rocky Mountains during the glacial period. If this highway was not so far from a population center, it would be an ideal sports car touring road (as long as drivers kept an eye out for sand in the corners).

I might need to come back here sometime and take a recon run in a sporty two-seater.

THRIVING

Making our way up Nebraska Highway 2, we stopped in the vibrant little town of Broken Bow. Its town square was hopping with activity—food trucks, craft sales, and the like. We'd stumbled onto Market on the Square, a summertime event held every Thursday. We walked a lap, then checked out the Custer County Museum and Research Center, on one side of the square. There we chatted with Tammy Hendrickson, a museum volunteer.

"Broken Bow was incorporated in 1887," Tammy explained. "The founders needed a name for the town so they could get a post office. Nobody could come up with a name they were satisfied with until some kids found an old Pawnee Indian bow that was broken. That's how the town got its name."

There were no trees and no railroad to deliver lumber, Tammy explained, so early settlers had to use whatever material they had at hand to build homes. This is the origin of the sod house, since there was no shortage of sod on the prairie. "There's still one of the original sod homes about 30 miles (48 kilometers) from here, which has survived all this time because the exterior had been stuccoed to preserve the structure."

CRAFT COFFEE PARLOR

120 N. MAIN STREET, MCPHERSON, KS 67460

Craft Coffee is a thriving coffee shop in this Kansas college town. Another excellent cortado served correctly with a sparkling water chaser!

Right: Little did we know when we visited Hastings, Nebraska, that we'd meet the town's new hero, Dylan Crawford. Two days earlier, Dylan, our server at Odyssey restaurant, had rescued an elderly couple from their burning home. He had been interviewed by all the area newspaper and television stations.

LOCAL HERO

Our young server at Odyssey was twenty-two-year-old Dylan Crawford, who had recently earned hero status in Hastings. A wrestling scholarship at Hastings College had brought him here from Lodi, California. For a brief time before his move, he had served as a police officer in Santa Cruz, but Hastings' wrestling coach had scouted the talented wrestler when Dylan was in high school and kept chasing him for years.

"I needed to get my degree, so after I married my girlfriend Jennica, we moved," he explained.

Dylan looks something like a young Kirk Douglas. Two days before we met, he'd proven his psychic relationship to that heroic screen idol. He and Jennica were enjoying their dinner from a taco truck in their townhouse's driveway. Glancing up from his burrito, "I saw fire at the house across the street," recalled Dylan. "I told Jennica to call 911, and I ran across the street." He knew an elderly couple with physical handicaps lived there.

"The doors and windows were locked, so I had to punch in the glass with my fists. The wife was in a wheelchair and was wheeling toward me, won-

dering what all the noise was. She didn't know her house was on fire. I grabbed her wheelchair and rolled her outside.

"Then the woman began yelling, 'My husband! My husband is in the bedroom!'"

Dylan ran back inside, found the husband in bed, and lifted him from there into his wheelchair.

"I didn't have his feet on the footrests, so he almost fell out of the chair a few times. I finally got the husband out, and he yelled, 'My dog is inside!'"

Dylan charged back into the burning house in search of the four-year-old boxer.

"The dog was frightened and wanted to bite me, so I took off my shirt and wrapped it around the dog's head. I said, 'Hey, buddy, it's either come with me or you're going to die.'"

He ran out with the dog in his arms as the roof collapsed behind him. It was only then that he felt burns on his back.

It was quite a day for the young wrestler and college student. His face was plastered all over the local paper and TV news. I asked Dylan what he thought his future held.

"Right now, that's totally up in the air. I blew my knee out wrestling, so I had to drop off the team. And my wife and I miss our families in California. So we'll probably move back there soon."

Certainly, a loss for Hastings, Nebraska.

Hastings felt like a happening town, likely helped by Hastings College. In addition to local heroes saving elderly residents from burning buildings, the town is also the birthplace of Kool-Aid, invented by local grocer and inventor Edwin Perkins in 1927. Sadly our timing was off to take in the annual Kool-Aid Days held each August.

In one of my former lives, I worked on Kool-Aid's public relations when they sponsored NASCAR driver Michael Waltrip in the Busch Grand National Series. My visit to Hastings made me feel like I'd come full circle—after only thirty years.

We visited Tank after dinner. True to the CTS driver's word, it was a dive. After a Bud Light (not my typical first choice), we got back in our rig and headed north on Highway 281 to our campground near Grand Island, Nebraska.

Right: Even though most people think of the great state of Nebraska as featureless, the Sand Hills offered some of the most beautiful vistas we'd seen, and the roads offered both high-speed curves and elevation changes.

I wondered how the town remained so active and kept up its population when other towns we'd passed seemed to be on their last legs.

"Well, we have two industries: agriculture and medical supplies. Becton, Dickinson and Company, based in New Jersey, manufactures medical vacuum tubes here. Their business is way up lately, and they're operating round-the-clock shifts seven days a week. Several hundred people work there, and they still need more. There's just not enough workers."

Sounds like the same issue the rest of the country has experienced since the start of the pandemic a few years ago.

DIVING

Getting back on the road, we next rolled through the village of Anselmo, also on Highway 2, northwest of Broken Bow. If that town was thriving, Anselmo looked to be *diving*. We stopped there to shoot a photo of a 1953 Chevy station wagon with a surfboard optimistically strapped on the roof.

"I bet the surfing around here sucks," I cracked to MAR as we made a U-turn back to the Chevy. A small, depressing main street started on the other side of the nearby railroad tracks.

Up main street, we met Tammy Burnett, the owner of Fubar & Grill, one of only two businesses operating on Anselmo's main drag. The other business is a tiny grocery.

"It's nice and quiet here," said the Haywood, California, native, who moved here after meeting her husband. "The town has about a hundred-and-forty residents today, but was once thriving."

As the railroads expanded, towns like Anselmo were built every 10 to 20 miles (16 to 32 kilometers) along the line. In the 1920s, Anselmo was a thriving community with a bustling downtown that included grain elevators, a roller mill, livery stables, restaurants, barber shops, five banks, and two newspapers.

These are the towns you imagine when you hear about kids who can't wait to grow up and leave for high-paying jobs in the big city. But not all kids. Tammy's seventeen-year-old son, Cameron, is about to enter his senior year of high school. He has other plans.

"I love math and I love carpentry. I've already built my mother a table and a dresser. I just love working with wood. We have a great industrial arts program in my school with a wood shop."

Remember when high schools had shop programs? There's an important message here.

"When I graduate, I want to do carpentry here in Anselmo."

Not everyone needs to be a marketing executive and live in a big city.

3.
THE NORTHERN SWING

THE ZEN OF NOT KNOWING WHAT'S NEXT

At 7 a.m. I walked into the KOA campground office in Hot Springs, South Dakota, where I was greeted by a nice lady behind the counter.

"Good morning," she said cheerfully. We exchanged pleasantries for a few minutes, and then I told her about our Florida-to-Alaska adventure. She asked where we'd been the day before, and I told her we had driven Highway 2 diagonally across Nebraska most of the day.

"Where are you going next?" she asked.

I had to think for a moment. I actually had no idea.

This was likely the first time since I was twelve years old that I had absolutely no agenda. Remember when you were a kid, and on a Saturday morning your friends met you on their bicycles and someone asked, "What do you want to do today?" and nobody had an answer?

That's how I felt. It was great.

Gone were the days when I had to rush off to meetings and meet project deadlines. Twenty years ago I sold a business and from that point to the present, I've been able to call my own shots. Long gone were the times I had to juggle a phone conference around showing up at my son's little league game.

I'm sure I'm not the only camper this lady had met who had no fixed agenda, but it was certainly a new experience for me.

"I don't really know," I told her, somewhat embarrassed.

But I've come to appreciate that the days with no definite beginnings have the very best conclusions.

"We'll just see what the new day brings," I said as I paid for two all-you-can-eat pancake-and-bacon breakfasts.

GOING, GOING...

We were outside Hot Springs, en route to some touristy places in western South Dakota, when something told me to look left after we crested a hill. And there it was: a Porsche. Sitting outdoors. On a piece or grass. Neglected.

Whaaaa?

As soon as I could turn the rig around, I drove back and up the steep driveway in front of the house. I knocked on the door. And waited. In a little bit, Doug Nikkila answered my knock.

"I bet people knock on your door every day asking about that car," I said.

"Well, not so much, but once in a while," admitted Doug.

He explained that it's not his car, that it belongs to his brother-in-law, John, who lives in Georgia.

"He's owned it for thirty years," he said. "He got it from his father. It was driven out here from Atlanta and parked. And it hasn't been cared for since."

Doug said the Porsche had been stored outdoors in nearby Sturgis, much of the time hidden behind shrubs.

"It was parked under a grapevine, and each summer when it bloomed, you couldn't even see the car," Dave recalled. "After John's parents passed, I moved the car here. It's been here for about four years."

Doug said John keeps it for sentimental reasons, even though a number of collectors have inquired about it over the years.

I gave the 912 a once-over. As can be imagined, any car that's been exposed to the elements for more than three decades—especially one as fragile as a nearly sixty-year-old Porsche—would normally qualify as yard art instead of a vehicle. Sitting here in Doug's yard, that's certainly what it had become.

The car had been the recipient of some poor bodywork in the past, with layers of fiberglass cloth lightly covering rot holes in the rocker panels. I saw evidence of four paint jobs. From the looks of it, the car had left Stuttgart in an ivory white color. It had also been painted a dark British racing green as well as orange before its last coat, a very pretty, very unoriginal light metallic blue.

The Porsche 912 was the four-cylinder variant of its more famous six-cylinder brother, the 911. The 912, the nine-hundred-and-twelfth Porsche engineering project, was the most direct descendent of the Porsche 356.

The car seemed complete: the interior was intact, most trim was in place, and, even though I couldn't lift the engine cover without possibly bending it, there looked to be the proper pancake engine in place. Even the original steel slotted wheels were present.

Until a few years ago, you couldn't give away a 912, especially one in rough condition. Those days are gone. Purists argue that the 912 is actually a better-balanced vehicle than the more tail-heavy 911. There has long been a small but ardent following for the 912, and word has gotten out: the 912 is a pretty darn good car.

John's car would probably rank as number 5 for condition, too rough to preserve and enjoy as is. Sadly the body tub was already compromised to the point where the passenger door wouldn't close because the structure was sinking in the middle. The door stayed shut thanks to a bungee cord.

With hourly restoration labor costs of $100 and up, plus parts and materials, paying to restore this car wouldn't have made sense ten years ago. But now, with a surge in interest and vaulting value, it might not put the new owner upside-down by the time he got it back on the road.

Let's hope that John's Porsche finds a worthy new caretaker, and that owner has the wherewithal to bring this important car back to its former glory.

AMAZING SITES AHEAD

I hope you'll allow us to be tourists for a little while this morning. Even though the mission of this trip has been to stay off the beaten path and visit sites seldom seen, sometimes you need to stop and smell the exhaust.

Our campsite in Hot Springs, South Dakota, is an hour away from a couple of amazing national wonders—but first, coffee commands MAR.

Above: Some landmarks are carved out of the natural land-scape, such as the nearby Mount Rushmore and Crazy Horse monuments. Others are created from manmade objects, such as this bicycle "sculpture" in the town of Pringle. Tourists can walk around and through the construction of hundreds, perhaps thousands, of two-wheelers.

In his continuing quest to discover the best coffee shop in America, MAR was pleased when an internet search for "best coffee shops in Hot Springs" highlighted Wandering Bison Coffee a mere 5 miles (8 kilometers) from our campsite. He has spoken lovingly of his doppio macchiato. And being less fussy, I thought my 24-ounce (700-milliliter) iced latte with oat milk offered a wonderful suggestion of, um, coffee. Plus it would likely keep me up all day and half the night.

PRINGLE—YOU CAN'T RIDE JUST ONE

Approaching our "tourist" destinations, we passed a little burg called Pringle. Somebody had to say it, and thankfully MAR did before I could get the words out of my mouth.

"I wonder if that's where Pringles potato chips were invented?"

But before I could give some wiseass answer, my eye landed on a site that could rival the World's Largest Ball of Twine—the Pringle Bicycle Pile. There was no sign or official name I could locate online, so let's say this is its official title for our purposes.

I did find a photo of a sign that identified the site as the "Midwest's Largest Bicycle Sculpture, And Possibly the World!" I'm sticking with "Pile."

Whatever you call it, it's a pile of hundreds, if not thousands, of bicycles, strategically stacked and wired together to form a sort of path under and through the bikes, like an immersive gallery. I saw old English racer-type bikes, newer road bikes, mountain bikes, and lots of little cildren's bikes. Most had badly bent wheels suggesting that they might have been damaged in road accidents, or maybe they were rejected by a bike rental company.

Regardless, it was interesting and strategically sited next to a bike trail.

Reviews on the internet ranked it 391 out of 460 places to see in South Dakota, and some called it a "monument" and a "hidden gem."

Honestly I'd rate it at least 378.

BIG SKIES AND BIG HEADS

The first place I wanted to visit in South Dakota was the Crazy Horse Memorial. Son Brian and I had passed through the Black Hills about fifteen years before on our California Surfing Safari. En route to Mount Rushmore, we stopped to take in the massive sculptural project.

WANDERING BISON

101 N. CHICAGO STREET, HOT SPRINGS, SD 57747

Wandering Bison is a great morning stop for a cappuccino. Since we visited, the owners have moved to a new, larger shop across the street. Business is good, for good reason.

Left: Eric and Laurie Cerroni experienced environmental and political changes they didn't care for in Utah, so they were in the process of moving their family to rural northern Minnesota when we met them at our Hot Springs, South Dakota, campground. Having lived with their three kids in a camping trailer for months, they were excited about reaching their new home in just a few days.

Right: We passed through Sturgis, South Dakota, and parked in front of the motorcycle museum, but we didn't go inside. Sturgis and its huge, annual motorcycle event have been well documented elsewhere. Our trip was about discovering lesser-known points of interest.

WANDERING BISON COFFEE, HOT SPRINGS, SD

Owners David and Heather Zortman have interesting back stories. Heather is a Detroit native who wanted to escape the Motor City's struggling economy. She moved to Wyoming in 2006, then to Hot Springs six years later.

"I saw the potential for a better life out West," said the forty-two-year-old. "I absolutely had more opportunity than I would have back home."

She and her children had settled in Wyoming until she met her soon-to-be husband, David, and moved to South Dakota to be with him.

A professional firefighter for the U.S. Forest Service, David leads a team of "Hotshots." He explained that Hotshots work on the ground, digging ditches, cutting clearings, and back-burning to contain the wildfires that he says are much more intense and frequent than when he began his career twenty years ago.

"We now have a higher level of training for when the shit hits the fan," he said. "I started firefighting in 1999, and the era of the megafire started in 2000, so I've seen it get worse over time."

David explained that there are over 100 Hotshot crews in the United States—about 2,100 firefighters dedicated to battling wildfires. They work very long hours during fire season. David, for example, will roll up 1,000 to 1,400 hours in overtime in just six months.

"I work fires in South Dakota, Idaho, Canada, and even Australia. But it's a young man's game, and I'm working on an exit strategy."

And that strategy is Wandering Bison Coffee.

"I worked in another coffee shop across town and decided that if I was going to work that hard, I might as well do it for myself," said Heather. "So we opened two-and-a-half years ago—right at the beginning of Covid. Fortunately we still had tourists and the business grew."

With confidence born of surviving and then thriving during the pandemic, Heather and David took the plunge and bought a building across the street from their current rented location.

"It had been a gas station, repair shop, a car dealership, and most recently a body shop," David told us as he proudly showed off his handiwork in building renovation. "We have big plans for more indoor seating, outdoor seating, and a drive-up window."

"We have a great customer base," said Heather. "We call out people by name when they walk into our shop. It's very much like a *Cheers* philosophy. It's all about quality ingredients, consistency, and creating a great atmosphere, where spontaneous conversations erupt among strangers."

A hard-working couple with nothing but blue skies ahead.

Left: I've visited Mount Rushmore on three occasions, and this is the scene that stops me in my tracks every time. It appears without warning while you approach on a side road to the visitors' center. George Washington's image manifests by itself through an opening in the surrounding trees—just breathtaking.

Below: MAR had me pose next to the four presidential faces, as if I was auditioning for an open spot on the mountain. This was after we'd had a few local craft brews at the visitors' center café. I know President Teddy Roosevelt was a big game hunter, but I'd be the only face up there who had hunted for *old cars*.

Right: What better way to wash down our lunchtime Buffalo Burgers than with Buffalo Snot beer? It's an oatmeal stout produced by the local Mt. Rushmore Brewing Company. Highly recommended.

"MOUNT RUSHMORE IS ETERNAL. IT WILL STAND UNTIL THE END OF TIME." — GUTZON BORGLUM, SCULPTOR

Today Crazy Horse's face is mostly complete, but work seems to have stalled over the decade and a half since I last visited the site. There is construction equipment on the mountain, but I don't think we'll see much progress in my lifetime. It does makes me wonder if the monument was designed to never be completed, instead meant to serve as a source of revenue, taking advantage of the traffic heading toward the Mount Rushmore National Memorial several miles away.

Whatever its state of completion, the sculpture's facial proportions are impressive: Crazy Horse's face is 87 feet (27 meters) tall and 58 feet (18 meters) wide. The forehead alone is 32 feet (10 meters) high and his nose is 27 feet (8.2 meters) long. The proposed height of the monument, when or if it is completed, is 563 feet (172 meters) high by 641 feet (195 meters) long. It's mind boggling to imagine.

Comparatively Mount Rushmore is all but finished. This monument is simply amazing and never fails to take my breath away, but it was never actually completed. Sculptor Gutzon Borglum's original intent was to carve full torsos, not just the heads of the four U.S. presidents depicted. This unfinished state is apparent from the roughed-out collar and lapels below George Washington's chin. Alas Borglum ran out of years before completing the project.

This was my third trip to see Mount Rushmore; the first was in the 1970s, then in the early 2000s, and now in 2022. The view that nearly brings me to tears is not the full four presidential faces. Instead it's the approach to the main parking area where, if you look at the right moment, President George Washington's face appears out of the rocky mountain between the tree branches. When Pat and I were driving cross-country in the 1970s, she passed the time reading the *AAA TripTik* tour book for the area. As we rolled through western South Dakota, she realized that we were not too far from Mount Rushmore. Callow youth that I was, I *reluctantly* agreed to stop and look at a bunch of heads carved into a mountain. But when we rounded that corner and I saw old George's face, I was blown away. This monument is worth a visit in your lifetime.

MAR and I decided to eat lunch at Mount Rushmore and sit outside on a deck below the famous carvings. What could be more American than eating a buffalo cheeseburger and washing it down with a Buffalo Snot beer from Mt. Rushmore Brewing Company?

FROM COLD TO COLDER

Back at our Hot Springs campground, we met a family on the cusp of a major life change. Eric and Laurie Cerroni, who had married right out of high school some eighteen years before, were moving with their three kids from Utah to northern Minnesota. The couple saw things happening in Utah that distressed them.

"We were just tired of all the fires and droughts out west. For us the new opportunities are in the North," explained thirty-six-year-old Eric.

Both Eric and Laurie had careers in the U.S. Army, he in artillery and she as an MP. Laurie left the service after her first stint to raise their three kids, but Eric stayed on until retirement. He then learned a new craft: butchering.

"We sold our house in Utah, paid off a lot of debt, and were able to buy a new house in Solway, near Bemidji, Minnesota."

Eric has already secured a job as a butcher, but noted that he's only a few credits shy of a bachelor's degree in biology, which he hopes will qualify him for a position with the Food and Drug Administration.

"But first things first," he said. "We've been living in our camping trailer for six months, and my kids really want their own space. We've got all our possessions in that U-Haul truck over there, and in three days we'll be in our new home."

Rather than remain in an environment that was deteriorating before their eyes, the Cerronis were taking control of their destiny. A bold move, and I appreciated their courage.

Left: This is one of my favorite images from the trip. We were driving just outside of Sturgis when MAR yelled, "Stop!" He saw the flat terrain in the foreground, the solitary mountain in the background, and the threatening clouds approaching. With the help of a drone, he nailed this shot!

Bottom: It was Memorial Day weekend, so we felt compelled to pay our respects at a military cemetery, in this case Black Hills National Cemetery. Standing in front of so many gravestones sent a chill through my body, and renewed my respect for the soldiers who fought and sacrificed for our country's freedom. Amen.

"GOOD THING YOU DIDN'T GET OUT OF THE CAR, BECAUSE HE'S A BITER. I'M SURPRISED THE COUNTY HASN'T MADE US PUT HIM DOWN."

PURE BEAN

201 MAIN STREET, THE CREAMERY BUILDING, RAPID CITY, SD 57701

Pure Bean was another amazing surprise when we least expected it. Excellent coffee craftsmen and everything done with care. I really wish we could have spent more time at this place. Worth a venture off the main highway.

A SOMBER MOMENT

It was Memorial Day weekend, so when MAR and I saw the Black Hills National Cemetery, we drove in pay our respects. The cemetery holds thousands of identical white headstones lined up in beautiful geometric patterns, like so many soldiers in formation.

People were visiting, leaving flowers, signs, and personal mementos for deceased soldiers they had known.

Moments like this get me choked up and make me glad I was born in America.

THE JUDGE AND THE CASE(S)

We passed through Sturgis, South Dakota, a quiet town—at least when the annual Sturgis Motorcycle Rally isn't choking its streets.

A few miles outside of town, though, we notice a yard full of orange tractors. Knowing that there must be a story here, we make one of our all-too-frequent U-turns and drive back to talk tractor.

We see a problem immediately. The house is about 100 feet from the road, and an unhappy barking dog is blocking our way to the front door. I was opening the Bronco's door to (hopefully) make friends with the dog when a woman walked out of the house.

"Get back in the truck!" she yelled. "He'll bite. I'll get him in the house."

MAR and I watched through the windshield while she wrangled her dog, who was clearly more interested in barking at us than going into the house. After a few minutes, Kathy Dykstra returned and introduced herself.

"Good thing you didn't get out of the car," she said, "because he's a biter. I'm surprised the county hasn't made us put him down. He's bad."

Glad not to have made his acquaintance, we introduced ourselves to Kathy. I asked about her impressive tractor collection.

"Those belong to my husband, Tom Huston. It all started when he attended a tractor pull with his brothers about 50 miles (80.5 kilometers) east of here. He said, 'Hmmm, this could be kind of interesting,' so he bought one at an auction. Then he said, 'If I only had a bigger one,' and now we have eighty of them."

Kathy explained that she and her husband used to live in Sturgis, but their growing tractor collection began to over-

whelm their neighborhood lot, so they decided a move to the country was in order.

"One tractor turned into two, and eventually five, and we just needed more room."

When they found a place out in the country with a big shed, they suddenly had all this room "and he just went nuts."

"First he collected Case tractors, then he started collecting all the models within a series. Then he started collecting plows and bailers and a windrowers, a rake, and a manure spreader."

Then Tom expanded into Farmall and Minneapolis-Moline tractors.

"And one John Deere," she added.

Walking around the property, I asked about the tractor pulling events. I'm probably naive, being from Long Island and all, but I thought tractor pulls employed custom-built tractors with nitro-powered funny car engines.

"The antique tractors don't make as much noise as the nitro tractors, but they require a lot more skill to drive, like which wheel brake to put on," she explained.

Of the eighty or so tractors the couple owns, some are for pulling, some for parts, some for collecting, and some are for actual farming. It sounded a lot like car collecting to me, apart from the farming.

"Kathy, can you drive a tractor?" I wondered.

"Oh, yes, I drive the propane tractors," she said. "They have a hand clutch. I can't drive those gas tractors with the foot clutches."

As we were about to leave, I saw something orange in the open garage behind the house.

"Is that a GTO?"

"Yes, it's my husband's Judge. He got it from his older brother when he was twenty. Now Tom is sixty-three years old."

As I inspected it, I realized it was a rare factory air conditioned car. The keys were in the GTO's trunk lock, so I gave them a twist and it opened. I immediately noticed that, though the exterior was orange, the trunk and rear bodywork indicated that it had left the factory in metallic green. I was suspicious that it might have been a "badge-engineered" Pontiac LeMans. But when I got home, I called my friends at Hagerty and they did a VIN search. Good news! The GTO is a genuine "two-door GTO hardtop coupe" originally finished in Verdero Green with black interior.

Sometimes you find a needle in a haystack, and sometimes you find an orange Judge among a bunch of orange Case tractors.

THE OTHER BIG SKY COUNTRY

Our occasionally straight, diagonal route from Florida to Seattle has taken on a somewhat unsightly wart as we make the essential turn into North Dakota.

We entered North Dakota at 5:26 p.m. on Saturday, May 26. It was cause for a minor celebration for both of us: the fiftieth state I had visited in my life and MAR's forty-eighth (he's missing only Alaska and Louisiana). We'd certainly need to celebrate at dinner that night. I was thinking a microbrew for myself, while MAR would probably have a cup of coffee, or a seltzer water, or some equally exciting beverage.

I know the Montana license plate slogan is Big Sky Country, and I don't mean to steal that from a state we had yet to visit, but good Lord: the sky is huge in North Dakota. Stories, photos, even movies can't do justice to the masterpiece we witnessed out our windshield. From horizon to horizon, as far as we could see—side-to-side, front-to-back—rolled a land without contour, seemingly infinite, not even a tree. It's immense and beautiful, like driving into a life-size Georgia O'Keeffe landscape.

Truthfully this was the part of the trip I'd been looking forward to the most. I've spent time in many parts of the country, for auto races, business trips, or just passing through. I've even spent a fair amount of time in Alaska. But I had never been to North Dakota, or driven this far north in the central United States.

If you live in, say, Brooklyn, or in a Virginia suburb of Washington, DC, or Miami or Atlanta, or Southern California, or some other densely populated urban center and want to give your brain a mental boost—and you can justify the time off and the resources to make it happen—get in a car and drive to this part of the country. I don't think you'll regret it.

It's like the first time I saw the Grand Canyon—I wanted to sit on the edge, meditate, and write poetry. Or something.

When I was a kid, I would occasionally ride with my mother to her work. Mom worked at a laboratory on the 4-to-midnight shift, and sometimes I'd go with her to swim in the pool or play basketball in the gym. Then I'd do my homework and go to sleep until her shift ended. I remember listening to a radio interview one night on the way home in which a scientist predicted that unless the world began to farm every square inch of available space—including the ocean floor—we would soon be unable to feed the world's population. Now, looking across North Dakota's vast open land about fifty-five years later, I can see how wrong that scientist was.

This is an amazing country.

TEST-DRIVING THE AIRSTREAAM

Before our rig was all lettered up, I tried out the Airstream Basecamp a few times because I'd never camped in a trailer before.

Well, that's not absolutely true. Joe and Marie Brischler, the parents of my lifelong friends Buzzy and Tommy, owned a little trailer they would park at Smith Point Park on Fire Island, about 20 miles (32 kilometers) from where I grew up in Holbrook, Long Island. They were nice enough to invite me to camp with them a couple of times. I could summarize my memories of these experiences like so: Buzzy and I made fried bacon sandwiches for breakfast and fried bologna sandwiches for lunch, and I learned that, if you let a lot of air out of your Schwinn Sting-Ray bicycle tires, you could ride your bike across the sand. That was the sum total of my trailer camping experience.

Thinking I might need a little more practice, I test-camped in the Basecamp 16X twice before MAR and I left for Florida. The first time was in my driveway. It

was interesting getting used to it, but I did get a decent night's sleep. A week later I tested it at a KOA campground about a half-hour north of my house. I wanted to experience hooking up the power and water lines and emptying the dump tank.

I made reservations, towed the trailer to the site, then unhitched it and drove home for dinner—not exactly adventure travel. When I returned, I set out a folding chair, opened a beer, and picked up where I left off reading Bill Bryson's *The Lost Continent*.

As I would quickly learn, a new Bronco pulling an unusual Airstream trailer attracts attention everywhere, especially in a campground. Within a few minutes, the gentleman parked next to me wandered over drinking a can of Milwaukee's Best.

"I like your rig."

I thanked him and described our upcoming trip, that we'd be leaving from Mile 0 in Key West and driving to the end of the road in Deadhorse, Alaska.

"What did you say about the end of the road?" he asked.

I told him that Deadhorse was on Prudhoe Bay, literally the end of the road in the United States.

"You got that right," he said. "I'm a flat-Earther, and that is the end of the road."

I was speechless. My mind was racing at 1,000 miles an hour. I wanted to debate him, about how is it all the water doesn't drain from the oceans and fall into space, about how the Sun and the Moon rise and fall in a circular motion over our heads, how the four seasons happen, had he ever traveled far from home, and so on. But I decided it was a discussion that likely would turn into an argument that couldn't be won.

I simply wished him a good night and went into my trailer to see if a quality night's sleep was possible in this newfangled trailer device.

RACING TO THE HAMPTON INN

It was Memorial Day Saturday, which meant tomorrow, Sunday, would be Auto Racing Day, USA. It has long been a tradition in the Cotter household, and in millions of U.S. households, to plant ourselves on the couch and snack away the entire day while watching the Formula One race in Monaco, the Indianapolis 500, and the Coca-Cola 600 at Charlotte Motor Speedway. But this year I'd be camping in a trailer without a TV set.

What to do?

The twenty-first-century answer: I posted a message on Facebook asking if anyone knew of a race watch party in central or western North Dakota. Sadly I received no serious results.

I had discovered the watch party concept while working in 2012 as president of a group attempting to bring Formula One racing to the New York City market (actually to the Jersey Shore along the Hudson River, with New York City as the backdrop). On Sundays, a group of loyal fans would wake up early and meet in any number of neighborhood pubs to begin drinking and eating before 7 a.m. on a Sunday morning. The New Jersey race never materialized, but I made a bunch of friends at these parties.

"What if we take a hotel room tonight in Bismarck?" I asked MAR. "We could take a break from camping, do our laundry, and I could watch the Monaco race?" MAR, though not the race fan that I am, had no problem with my scheme.

We booked a room at the Hampton Inn in Bismarck and enjoyed a brief reprieve from camping, two real beds, a full-size shower, and a non–peanut butter sandwich dinner.

Memorial Day Sunday was a lazy event. As opposed to other mornings when we were awakened by fellow campers preparing to depart on their own road trips, we were able to sleep late, like 7:30 a.m. Real beds felt pretty darn nice.

I enjoyed the Grand Prix, which started an hour late because of rain. It was a good race, won by my favorite driver, Sergio Perez in the Red Bull car, over Carlos Sainz in the Ferrari. Perez' teammate Max Verstappen finished third.

Because the race started an hour late, it wrapped up close to 11 a.m., perfect for our checkout time. We packed up and hit the road, setting our sights on Highway 2. My Cobra-owning friends Dan and Martha Case live in Montana, and they'd suggested this east-west route along the Canadian border was both remote and a likely stretch on which to spot old cars.

Highway 2 connects eleven states across the northern U.S., beginning in Houlton, Maine, and running all the way to Washington State. It measures 2,575 miles (4,144 kilometers) in length, but the route is not contiguous through the United States. The highway's eastern and western segments are connected by a series of Canadian roadways, as designed in the path's original 1926 plans. We could grab Highway 2 north of Bismarck and take it all the way to Washington and the Pacific Ocean. That's my kind of two-lane road!

IF DOT'S PRETZELS ARE RELIGION, GOING TO THE DOT'S NORTH DAKOTA FACTORY IS LIKE VISITING THE VATICAN.

THE TROUBLE WITH DOT

I had totally sworn off Dot's Pretzels, but when I saw bags of the wicked product at a convenience store where we refueled, I had to buy some for MAR, who had never tried them.

"Try these," I slyly invited when I got back into the car. He took a small handful.

"Cotter, you son of a bitch," he said of the magical twists of salty goodness. "These things are like crack!"

In case you've never tried Dot's, go slowly. They're addictive.

You can get Dot's in many grocery stores now, but that hasn't always been the case. I bought my first bag of these while in an Ace Hardware store in Maine several years ago. I was there for some tubes of Flex Seal. I noticed bags of Dot's Pretzels displayed next to the checkout counter.

"Are these any good?" I asked the saleslady.

"They're addictive," she warned.

I grabbed a bag and ate nearly all of it on the way home; and I only lived five minutes away! I was hooked.

When I returned home to North Carolina at the end of the summer, I stumbled in, pretzel seasoning smearing my face and hands. My wife read the ingredients and told me the pretzels were very high in sodium and contained MSG, so I tried to take it easy. And sought counseling.

Come Super Bowl Sunday that year, I went to the local Ace Hardware to buy a couple of bags for our little game-day party. I asked the lady behind the counter how they were selling that day.

"More people are coming in for pretzels today than for nuts and bolts."

Clearly I was not alone. Now I try to partake of them in limited amounts, only on special occasions. Like when I'm watching the Super Bowl. Or an auto race. Or when I'm in North Dakota.

You see, Dot's founder, Dorothy Henke, manufactures the little buggers in Velva, North Dakota. Name me another nationally available consumer product that originates in North Dakota.

If Dot's are religion, going to the Dot's factory is like visiting the Vatican. We had to go. We could fill the back of the Bronco with samples.

We found the address and drove to a surprisingly small commercial building near the center of the very small town of Velva. How could such a small facility satisfy a country full of Dot's diehards?

After checking the company's website, I discovered how they produced enough of the seasoned little rascals to keep America happy. They contract with bakeries in Arizona and Kansas to help satisfy demand. And those bakeries are silent regarding Dot's secret ingredients.

LOCAL RACING

All along the trip that day, to Velva and beyond, we listened to the Indianapolis 500 on the Bronco's SiriusXM satellite radio. I must admit that I wasn't familiar with the winning driver, Marcus Ericsson, but I felt happy for team co-owners Chip Gannasi and my friend, Rob Kauffman. In my heart I was hoping that either Hélio Castroneves or Tony Kanaan, both veterans, would be triumphant.

The plan was to listen to the radio broadcast of the Coca-Cola 600, being broadcast from my home track in Charlotte that evening, but a funny thing happened on the way to the forum . . .

In Jack Kerouac's book *On the Road*, Dean Moriarty habitually visits small racetracks as he crisscrosses the country in a constant state of drug and alcohol intoxication. I had told MAR early in the trip I had hoped to visit a small-town, short track race—albeit sober—at some point before we reached Deadhorse, though I realized that might not work out. Then we passed a county fairground as we drove into Minot, North Dakota.

Left: I first picked up a bag of Dot's Pretzels while buying Flex Seal at my local Ace Hardware store. Eventually that was my connection for buying Dot's Pretzels and, oh, hardware too. We stopped in Velva, North Dakota, at the Dot's headquarters, hoping to interview Dot herself. Sadly the company was closed on Memorial Day, so we comforted ourselves with a bag of Original Seasoned— at a nearby Ace Hardware.

First I noticed race car transporters pulling into the Nodak Speedway parking lot. Then I saw the fateful sign: "Racing Tonight!"

"Michael, we need to go to there!" I exclaimed.

It had been years since I'd gone to a local short track race. And MAR had never been to one.

Minot, the fourth-largest city in North Dakota, with a population of about 50,000 today, was historically the northernmost trading post on the U.S. side of the Canadian border. It is best known for the Minot Air Force Base, 15 miles (24 kilometers) from town. In the 1920s Minot's downtown grew rapidly, and with that growth came crime: bootlegging, prostitution, opium dens. The city earned the nickname "Little Chicago."

In more modern times, the town has become a destination for racers and race fans. As was once a fairground tradition, a racetrack is but one part of a fairground complex that might otherwise host a cattle auction or rodeo. The track in Minot is ³/₈ of a mile (.6 kilometer) long with a surface of dirt—not red clay like I was used to in the Carolinas, but damp dirt. The track hosts classes for Modifieds, Stocks, Compacts, and Sport Mods.

I asked at the credentials office who I might talk to about gaining access to the paddock area, and which race driver would be a worthy story for me to highlight in this book. I was connected with Brandon Beeter, who informed me that he runs the track's all-volunteer racing organization.

Brandon steered me to veteran racer Mike Hagen, a multiple-time track champion, whose son Travis is following in his father's footsteps.

"Sounds good, I'd love to meet them," I told Brandon. We walked through the prerace activity in the pits to a location next to the fence where the Hagens have parked for years.

Mike is from Williston, North Dakota, two hours west of Minot. He's fifty-seven years old and has been racing at Nodak Speedway for thirty-one years. His wife Nadine accompanies her husband each Sunday, "May 1st through Labor Day," she says.

"Mike and I have been together for thirty-three years, so I've been coming to the races with him that long. We pretty much raised our kids at the racetrack. The cars are safe. I've never worried about any of my family."

"This is our family activity," explained Mike, who has so many championships that he's lost count, but knows his first was in 1992.

His son Travis is thirty-one years old. He began racing International Motor Contest Association (IMCA) Modifieds nine years ago and has chalked up an impressive eight championships.

Left: Mike has raced for thirty-one of fifty-seven years he's been around. He sponsors his #27 Chevelle stock car himself with the profits from his seed-cleaning business. The night we were there, he won the race and pocketed the $750 first prize. Son Travis also won his race in a higher division and made $1,000. Both admitted the winnings would barely be enough to cover tires and the fuel to commute from their homes in Williston, South Dakota, to Minot and back.

Below: We connected with a racing family, the Hagens, who live in Williston, about two hours west of Minot. Here Travis Hagen prepares wife Makenzie's race car before working on his own. Travis' father Mike is the auto racing family's patriarch.

Right: For millions of Americans, there is no more patriotic activity on Memorial Day weekend than to cook hot dogs and hamburgers on a grill, get together with friends and family, and attend an auto race. By chance we found ourselves in Minot, North Dakota, home of Nodak Speedway, a 3/8-mile (.6-kilometer) dirt track. We quickly canned plans to watch Charlotte's Coca-Cola 600 on TV and obtained a couple of pit passes.

MIddle: Race promoter Brandon Beeter told me he was satisfied with the size of the crowd on this Memorial Day Sunday race. Between 1,500 and 1,700 fans came to the fairgrounds racetrack to celebrate America's greatest day of auto racing.

Bottom: Son Travis in Victory Lane. Wife Makenzie, holding son Revvin, walks to meet Travis during post-race interviews. Travis sells race car parts to racers like himself for a living; winning helps promote his parts business.

Obviously the wrench didn't fall too far from the tool bench. Even Travis' wife, Makenzie, swaps off between holding the couple's son, Revvin, racing in the #10 IMCA Sport Mod class against an all-male field.

"We don't have Powder-Puff Derbies for the girls here," noted Nadine.

Between his own racing heats in his #14, Travis was juggling rear ends: changing the gears in Makenzie's car and then changing Revvin's diapers.

For the past three years, Mike has been racing the #27 IMCA Chevelle Stock, which has about 500 horsepower. It resembles the plastic model kits many of us assembled as kids, covered with stickers from local sponsors who pitch in money or parts to support Mike's program. The dashboard features photos of his family's three springer spaniel dogs and their two cats. One of those dogs, Moxie, was in attendance at the race we saw. He was obsessed with his rubber ball that I made the mistake of throwing for him. And throwing. And throwing.

One of the sponsor decals on the race car was for Mike's seed cleaning company. As a native New Yorker, I had to plead ignorance. Seed cleaning? "I clean grain for farmers, mostly seeds for lentils, beans and durum wheat, which goes into pasta," he explained. His company literally separates the wheat from the chaff, making the seed easier to store and distribute and cutting down on the possibility of disease. "I bring my truck onto a farm, clean the seeds, then move on."

That night's race was Mike's first of the season. "It's good to be back. It's my first time racing this season because of the bad weather we've had this spring. I'm pretty much the old-timer, and have known most of these other drivers since they were kids."

Racing on a banked track coated with moist, slick dirt would be like driving as fast as possible during a snowstorm for the rest of us. The pack of cars race on extremely soft, cross-check-pattern tires inflated to only 10 or 15 psi and slide at a 45-degree angle to the track walls when cornering. Organized chaos or "roller derby on ice" would accurately describe the racing, regardless of which class. If you tried this with your street car during a blizzard, you'd surely hit the object nearest the apex, jack your insurance rates, and land your car in the body shop for three months. But here it's all just racin'.

It was fun to watch, and promoter Brandon Beeter seemed pleased with the turnout of about 1,500 or so spectators.

Tonight's race pays the winner of Mike's class $750. After a couple of heat races, Mike will start on the pole. When the green flag falls, he shot out in front of the rest of the field. He had clearly mastered the art of sideways. He'd be your guy in a blizzard.

Before the race I had asked Nadine why she wore a "Mad Mike Hagen" T-shirt when her husband seemed like a pussycat during the few hours I had spent with him. "It's his bad temper," she warned.

During Mike's race, the father-and-son team of Joe and Joey Flory, who drove equally fast cars, seemed to gang up on Mike, cutting him off and trying to spin him out. Seemingly every lap had a different leader as the three drivers swapped positions. After twenty laps of "banging and pranging," as the late Dale Earnhardt Sr. called it, Mike came home the winner.

Albeit a mad winner.

An argument ensued in the pits at postrace inspection, but not between him and the Florys: the target of Mike's wrath was Joe Flory's wife. Cuss words flew from both corners, then Joe and Joey showed up. Thankfully nothing physical took place; crew members wisely got between the warring drivers and prevented an altercation. But as Mike and I walked to his trailer, he smiled. He wasn't so mad after all.

"But my car wasn't dented before, and now it's dented," he said. "So next race, watch out!"

Mike took home the $750 purse, which he said would about cover the cost of four new tires and the round-trip fuel costs from home to the track and back.

The last race of the evening, the feature race for Travis's Modified class, had a $1,000 payday for the win. By this time in the evening, the drivers were searching for the darker, damp dirt on the track, which had worked its way up the banking as the racing progressed. The track was drying out, and as the fast race cars rotated around the tight circuit, the dust in the air eventually turned into clods of dirt. There

was sure to be a decrease in water pressure tonight in Ward County as everyone sought to wash off the track's soil they'd collected on themselves.

MAR wanted to shoot photos of the feature race, but he quickly reconsidered as he tried to protect his valuable camera gear from the dust and dirt-filled air.

Travis dominated his race from beginning to end, winning the $1,000 prize. "My son is a lot better driver than I ever was," admitted Mike. "He's smarter and more calculating."

The Hagen family had the best weekend they could imagine this Memorial Day Sunday, with combined purses of $1,750 and two of their three cars in the winner's circle.

As Michael and I were preparing to leave after one heck of a good time, I asked Makenzie if her infant son might represent the Hagen family's third generation of race drivers.

"With a name like Revvin, I'm not sure he has a choice."

So we saw the Monaco Grand Prix on the hotel TV, listened to the Indy 500 on the Bronco's radio, but totally missed the Coca-Cola 600 NASCAR race from Charlotte Motor Speedway.

We made up for that by celebrating Memorial Day at a local dirt track race with a family who invited us into their lives for the evening. There was a little racing, a little cussing, and a little fighting. But there were also smiles, laughter, and hot dogs. And after the races, beer. Isn't that the way family holidays should be spent in two-lane America?

NODAK FIELD WORK

After the races, we retired to our Airstream and camped at the RoughRider Campground, owned by the local RV Center.

Top right: Never expecting to find a field full of old cars on Memorial Day Monday, we stumbled upon Dick's Auto in Minot, just a few miles west of Nodak Speedway. I knocked on the door of the adjacent house and Dick himself answered. We spent the next couple of hours poking around his inventory. I was instantly attracted to this 1950 Mercury, one of the most desirable sedans for collectors and hot rodders alike. James Dean drove one in the movie *Rebel Without A Cause*, and customizer George Barris became famous by building versions that were featured on magazine covers in the 1950s.

Bottom right: Something you don't see every day: a 1953 Kaiser Manhattan four-door sedan. Surprisingly sound and nearly complete, this would be an ideal starting point for an unusual resto-mod, featuring a stock interior and a modern drivetrain. Dick's asking price? $2,000.

Independent campgrounds can be something of a hit-or-miss proposition. Though most mom-and-pop campgrounds are extremely clean and well managed, once in a while you get a clinker. The RoughRider Campground was excellent, with some of the cleanest bathrooms and showers we'd seen.

We left town still driving west on Highway 2, and within a few miles passed a field of cars too good to miss.

"Pull over, Michael!"

What had been a single rusty Ford pickup soon appeared as a field of cars and trucks. Once we were on the property, the car count looked close to 200. We had stumbled across Dick's Auto.

As a boy I had discovered the art of finding old cars by reading *Rod & Custom Magazine*'s Vintage Tin column. I was a hot rod–crazy kid from Long Island, jealous of the variety of old cars my western counterparts could get their hands on. It seemed like every farm in the West had a field of old cars behind the barn. The field that comprised Dick's Auto reminded me of the images I had seen on those pages fifty years before.

My rule after spotting an old car or cars is to park mine out in the open, never wishing to appear underhanded. Then I walk around with my hands in my pockets. To date my theory has worked, having never been shot at and seldom run off, and bitten by only one dog. So we parked the Bronco and Airstream, stuck our hands in our pockets, and took a stroll through the field.

It was obvious that Dick's was a commercial establishment, but this being Memorial Day Monday, it probably wasn't open. I wondered if the house at the end of the long driveway might be Dick's?

"Michael, I'm going to knock on the door of that house," I said, not knowing if the occupants were home on this holiday. But Dick answered the door and gave us permission to look at his inventory. "Come on back over when you're done," he invited.

Michael and I spent the next forty-five minutes shooting photos of trucks and cars, mostly from the 1950s through the 1970s. Then we knocked on Dick's door again.

Dick's Auto is run by Dick and his wife Nancy. Dick handles the automotive inventory—buying, selling, transporting—and Nancy manages the paperwork, titles, and website updates. Dick and Nancy Sundhagen appeared to be quite the productive team.

"Cars are my life," said Dick. "My father was a farmer who knew where all the old cars were."

Dick and Nancy were a well-oiled machine, where one could seamlessly finish the other's sentences, as only long-married partners can manage.

Dick was determined to make cars his life's work, so out of high school he enrolled in an auto body school in Minnesota, where he met Nancy. He opened a body shop, but ultimately decided that the antique car business was really how he wanted to spend his time.

"I sold the body shop twenty-eight years ago and started selling Model Ts," he said. "Now I sell a couple of hundred cars a year."

Dick calls it a hobby business, but I know it's more serious than that.

Top Left: The car I first noticed as we drove past on Highway 2 from Minot was this rare 1960 Oldsmobile Super 88 "Bubble Top." As a two-door hardtop, this is the sportiest body style Oldsmobile manufactured that year. Dick offers this car with a clean North Dakota title for $4,000.

Bottom left: Once the desire of every Hollywood star and starlet—and the name of a Bruce Springsteen song—this pink Cadillac is parked at Dick's Auto, waiting for someone to take it home and give it some love. I'm guessing that salt is not dumped on winter roads in North Dakota, because the cars at Dick's have surprisingly little rust.

Right: The team behind the success of Dick's Auto, Dick and Nancy Sundhagen, run the entire operation. Dick scouts out cars, transports, and sells, while Nancy secures titles and updates the company website. It's obviously working, because they have customers throughout the United States and around the world.

From their rural location west of Minot, they've done business with people from around the world, some of them famous.

"So far we've shipped cars and trucks to new owners in thirty-nine foreign countries," Nancy said. "We even sold a 1956 Chevy to Jennifer Lopez as a gift for her cousin." She added that most of their business is from their website, but in the summer they sometimes get tourists stopping by after spotting their inventory from the road.

Dick's has also provided vehicles for movies and TV shows, such as *American Horror Story* and *Swamp Hunters*. And the national restaurant chain Texas Roadhouse bought a bunch of their pickup trucks.

The couple showed me a recent local newspaper story that noted: "Right now they have fourteen cars and trucks going to Thailand, two to the U.K., and two to Australia."

Nancy said that Dick is "like the Godfather. When our local car club has a meeting or cruise-in, people wait in line to talk to Dick."

How does he do it? What's Dick's secret to finding so many old cars?

"The cars find me," he explained. He said people contact him when they want to sell an old car or find old cars. The day before we stopped by, Dick had purchased a group of cars from an estate sale. The Sundhagens were preparing to collect them as soon as we left.

I wondered what cars were their best sellers? "Pickup trucks, especially Chevys, 1947 to 1953, 1970s and 1980s," said Dick. "Everyone wants a short-bed Chevy, but they just didn't sell them around here. We're all farmers out here, and we needed long-bed work trucks. If I could find a hundred short-bed Chevys right now, I'd buy them."

Dick shared a story about an Arizona customer. "He bought a 1948 Ford pickup from us with no heater and he wanted to drive it home. The outside temperature was −26°F (−32° C). I advised him against it, because the truck's top speed was only 45 miles per hour (72 kilometers per hour). What if he broke down?"

The intrepid buyer eventually made it back to Arizona. To top it off, a few years later the same guy, driving the same truck, stopped by Minot on his way to Newfoundland.

I wondered if Dick and Nancy had any old cars they *wouldn't* sell. Their keeper is a 1948 Chevrolet Suburban that their son built for them. Soon after its completion, he passed away from brain cancer. "It's our daily driver."

My original guess of 200 vehicles on their property? I was off by a factor of two!

A cool couple who happily greeted your two faithful adventurers on a holiday morning. I was so happy to have met them.

A BEER WITH A STORY

Our original plan was to visit a cool coffee shop each morning and an equally cool microbrewery in the evening, but in an effort to cut down on my beer consumption, brewery visits were less frequent than coffee runs.

That noted, while heading west along Williston's old downtown Main Street, we happened upon a tavern featuring a novel, yet time-honored, service model. Hops & Berry Taproom offers a large beer selection and a limited food menu—and the beer is self-serve.

This was new concept for me. It operates like the old Horn & Hardart Automats that first appeared in post–World War I New York City and Philadelphia and saw their heyday in the 1940s and 1950s. I gave the man behind the counter, Carson Hatter, a credit card and he gave me a sort of key fob. I could then pour my own beer from any of the multiple wall-mounted beer and wine taps. A computer tracked how many fluid ounces each of us drank and the tally was charged to my card. The beer selection was arranged by style: stouts, lagers, pilsners, IPAs, and so on. A fun approach.

Food was limited to wings, potato skins, and such, the types of foods easily prepared by a non-chef. I asked Carson how folks liked the concept, how much traffic there was, and were there any other locations. Turns out the taproom is owned by an attorney based in Atlanta, and Hops & Berry is one of several local businesses he owns in Williston. Local staff manage the various properties.

The twenty-one-year-old Carson grew up in and around Williston. "From third grade until I was a senior in high school, I went to school in nearby Trenton. It's a native community, run by the Turtle Mount Chippewa. I was the only white kid in the school."

Carson explained that the area was settled predominantly by Norwegian and Swedish immigrants, while his ancestors were Irish. "I grew up in the minority in almost every situation in my life."

Carson has an actor's handsome looks, or perhaps those of a 1970s rock musician who might have played guitar for

the Doobie Brothers. He said he had the opportunity to go to college, even some scholarship offers, but decided that college wasn't really his thing. "It just wasn't in my bones." He worked in IT for a Minnesota company for a couple of years because he felt Williston was never going to change.

"When I was growing up, Williston was a tiny town. The scenery never changed."

Then huge oil reserves were discovered in 2008 and everything *did* change.

"They struck oil—a lot of it," Carson explained. "You could make six figures if you moved here. But that's when things changed. When I was a kid, my mom told me to be home when the streetlights came on—suddenly there was drugs, crime, human trafficking.

"Fifty hotels went up. There weren't enough places to live for all the people that were moving in. When the price of oil dropped ten years later, many of those hotels came down.

"During the boom years, my dad made $90,000 a year as a safety inspector working two weeks on, two weeks off."

Carson moved home and got into the oil business himself, making $25 an hour working in IT for an oil company. But that wasn't in his bones either.

"I play guitar and piano, so I joined a band that sounded good enough for drunk people, but not sober ones," he laughed.

"Williston is just an oil town, and it will never be anything else. It's strange, because oil's the only thing going on here, nothing else. Well, oil and coffee shops." MAR's ears perked up at that. "There are a shit-ton of them in this town, most of them drive-up booths."

He said that women in Williston were expected to be stay-at-home housewives because their husbands all made six-figure salaries.

JESUS SAID THE MEEK WOULD INHERIT THE EARTH,
BUT SO FAR ALL WE'VE GOTTEN IS MINNESOTA
AND NORTH DAKOTA.
– GARRISON KEILLOR

Opposite, left: Our bartender in Williston, North Dakota, Carson Hatter, grew up in that town, but he can't wait to leave. Looking like a rock musician, or perhaps a younger version of Peter Fonda, he believes that there are many more opportunities elsewhere and vows to move—as soon as he gets a few more tattoos.

Opposite, right: Like Carson Hatter, Carly Thomas grew up in Williston, but unlike him she never wants to leave. She loves her job, loves the town, and travels to far-off vacation spots like Hawaii. She's an ideal restaurant server who kept us informed and engaged.

Right: After the unmoving traffic jam at Dick's Auto, we were on the road, headed west on Highway 2. This is how the road appeared for the next several days.

"Williston is not for young people," lamented Carson, "because there isn't much to do here except get drunk."

I could tell Carson was depressed with his station in life. He admitted he was looking forward to leaving, but only one thing was holding him back.

"It'll probably be Colorado. It's been my favorite destination. Maybe Colorado Springs, because it's cheaper than Denver. But first I need to visit a tattoo artist in town I really like. After he tattoos my arms, I'm leaving. And I'm not coming back."

"I thought I'd buy a van and soup it up," he said. "I could live out of it for a couple of years. I'll travel light, and between bartending and my IT work, I think I'll make it."

I wished Carson well, and I really hope he makes it out of Williston.

ROUGHING IT — SORT OF

So far we'd camped in KOA and independent campgrounds, but we wanted to explore further options, so we decided to boondock in a Walmart parking lot a few miles from the Hops & Berry Tavern.

"Boondocking" is camping without the traditional hookups of electrical, water, and sewage. With our little Basecamp 16X, which lacks a generator, that meant no air conditioning and no heat. In Florida, no AC would have been uncomfortable. But in Williston, with a nighttime forecast in the mid-50s (about 10°C), we didn't think there would be a problem.

Some research confirmed that Walmart does allow camping in its parking lots, except where prohibited by local ordinances. With over 4,000 Walmarts nationwide, though, roughly 50 percent still offer parking-lot camping.

This was certainly a wise business move. The stores have huge, well-lit parking lots that are mostly empty overnight. Making them available to campers ensures a lot full of customers each morning. And it makes campers loyal to the Walmart brand.

Luckily the Williston Walmart allowed camping, so we tucked our rig in the corner of the parking lot near the garden center. We were bordered on one side by flowers, bales of mulch, and a stack of wheelbarrows, and on the other side by fellow campers. The scenery could be worse.

With the Basecamp set up for our boondock experiment, we moseyed over to Doc Holliday's Roadhouse, a restaurant owned by a local family. It had the rustic look of a traditional western steakhouse like you might expect in an oil boomtown, and it was named after the infamous American gunfighter of the late 1800s whose occupations also included gambling and dentistry. Out front stood a row of life-size bronze horses. The beer selection was adequate, and the food was decent, but the best thing about our dining experience was our bright-eyed server.

Carly Thomas was eight years old when her dad got a job in the oil industry and moved the family from Colorado to Williston. Carly's story was the opposite of Carson Hatter's, the server we'd met a few hours before.

"I HAVE ALWAYS SAID I WOULD NOT HAVE BEEN PRESIDENT HAD IT NOT BEEN FOR MY EXPERIENCE IN NORTH DAKOTA." — THEODORE ROOSEVELT

"My dad worked for Halliburton as a frac hand, during the first oil boom," said the twenty-two-year-old. "There was so many people moving to Williston that there weren't enough places to live, but people just said 'fuck it' and moved here anyway. Entire families were living in tent cities, even in the wintertime."

Her father bought a house in town for $175,000 and saw it double in value within a few years.

Despite the commotion of living in an overpopulated city, Carly clearly loves Williston.

"This is my home," she said. "My boyfriend and I just bought a townhouse together."

And she's pleased with her job at Doc Holliday's as server manager.

"I make good money, which allows me to travel. I've been to Utah, Texas, Hawaii. I'd rather live here and make good money than live in Colorado and barely make enough money to survive."

THE NODAK LONG VIEW

"I've been coming to work in this building for forty-six years," said Wayne Lund, "and I've owned the business for the past fifteen."

Before we left Williston, I wanted to meet someone whose fortunes rose and fell with the boom-and-bust oil industry. Wayne was the perfect candidate.

"Modern Machine Works is the oldest machine shop in town," Wayne said. "Between 1980 and 2008, we had twenty-one machinists employed here. Then the oil business fell, and we were down to four employees."

With his long, white beard and stout belly, sixty-five-year-old Wayne looks more like Santa Claus than a machinist. He worked his way up to owner the old-fashioned way: starting at the bottom. From his time as an entry-level welder, he learned the other parts of the business, and he and his wife Betty eventually bought the shop.

"The demand for my services gets stronger and lesser with the oil industry," Wayne explained. "I've never worked on an oil rig myself, but I've worked with every piece of one in the shop. The oil industry is about 90 percent of our business. The rest is welding broken farm equipment and even fixing office chairs."

As Wayne recalled, "It used to take twenty to thirty days to drill a hole two and a half miles deep. Today they can go that deep in five days. They can even drill sideways. And when the companies are fracking, they're pushing mud down into the ground at 30,000 pounds of pressure, which pushes oil to the surface."

Wayne doesn't really travel, having only gone once to Nashville and Chicago each. He fondly recalls the Williston of old.

"When I was in high school, it was a sleepy little town. Agriculture was the main industry. Farming is still big around here, but now those farmers have built big houses on the edge of town because they sold the mineral rights below their fields."

When oil was discovered in the late 1980s, Wayne said there was an increase in violent crime, like shootings. "And more transient workers moved in without places to live."

"The cost of living increased for all of us—the price of food, gas. When oil was booming, there were 120 rigs in operation. Now forty-one rigs are operating. The problem here is when oil goes bust, the prices for consumer products don't go down. That's when it gets rough."

I wasn't surprised to learn that Wayne plays Santa Claus at Christmastime. He's been featured on the local NBC station and has entertained children in nearly every store in Williston, including visits to about a dozen houses each Christmas Eve.

"I'll deliver the family's Christmas presents and bring candy canes and trinkets." Even when the temperature is −53°F (−47°C), as it was for one recent Christmas.

"I love seeing the kids smile," he says.

As we continued our trek west and approached the Montana state line, I reflected on time well spent in North Dakota. We'd met a fascinating variety of people—race drivers, restaurant servers, a collector-car dealer, and a machinist who doubles as Santa Claus—all of whom had shared their stories with us. It was exactly as I had hoped when planning this road trip months earlier—better actually. I couldn't wait to cross that next state line.

4.
CROSSING AND CROSSING AND STILL CROSSING MONTANA

Left: Welcome to our twelfth state, Montana. I'd visited a couple of times in the past, but had never traveled this far north. Our route on Highway 2 would parallel the Canadian border all the way to Washington.

THE TIME ZONES THEY ARE A CHANGIN'

We entered Montana on Tuesday, May 31, at 12 p.m. Central Time and the clocks on our iPhones switched immediately to Mountain Time. Suddenly it was 11 a.m. again. I felt younger and relished the opportunity to correct all my errors of the previous hour.

My phone's GPS told me we were still more than 1,000 miles (1,609 kilometers) away from Seattle. What I thought was the smell of the Pacific Ocean was probably more cow manure. The Bronco's trip odometer registered 3,895 miles (6,268 kilometers), so I suspect we'll hit 5,000 miles (8,050 kilometers) by the time we reach Seattle where we'll park the rig and take an extended pit stop.

Not wanting to make the same mistake as when we entered Nebraska, neglecting to pay respect to Bruce Springsteen's song of the same name, we began reciting the lyrics to Frank Zappa's *Moving to Montana Soon*—at least those we could remember.

I've been to Montana in the past for a few short visits: a Cobra Tour, *Barn Find Hunter* episodes, and crossing the state on cross-country runs. But I hadn't ventured as far north on my previous trips to the state.

WOLF POINT HIGH POINTS

Wolf Point, Montana, is about 75 miles (120 kilometers) west of the North Dakota border. We stopped at the museum there and met volunteer and recent Montana transplant Sandy Woodstock. To learn about her newly adopted town, Sandy was reading Marvin Presser's *Wolf Point, A City of Destiny*.

Ranching and farming are the area's main industries. The key crops are wheat, flaxseed, hemp, and barley, the latter mostly grown for Anheuser-Busch. Sandy said that living near the Fort Peck Indian Reservation created a very different atmosphere from her former life in the Midwest. "I've never experienced two forms of government before, Indian and American."

Another museum volunteer, Sarah Wagner, told us more about the Wild Horse Stampede rodeo. "It's held on the second weekend of July, and it's the main moneymaker for our town. Plus, Wolf Point is the only place to shop within 100 miles."

Sarah is twenty-five-years old. She was born and raised in Wolf Point and has devoted considerable time to studying the town's history. "The town was established in 1915, but people started to settle here as early as the 1880s," she said. "Lewis and Clark came through here as they were heading west in 1805. They were following the Missouri River, which is a mile (1.6 kilometers) away. They came through again on their return voyage a year later. Before Lewis and Clark, fur traders from Canada went trapping throughout the area. It was a major hub for trading."

Below: MAR's drone accurately captured the landscape in northeastern Montana. The scenery's openness enhanced its understated beauty. Taking in the full view, you might notice what appears to be the earth's slight curvature.

"I'M IN LOVE WITH MONTANA. FOR OTHER STATES, I HAVE ADMIRATION, RESPECT, RECOGNITION, EVEN SOME AFFECTION. BUT WITH MONTANA IT IS LOVE."
— JOHN STEINBECK, *TRAVELS WITH CHARLEY*

Top: We occasionally visited local museums during the trip to get a feel for the areas we passed through. This one in Wolf Point, Montana, was a small-town museum that featured locally used or developed implements, household items, and building techniques. Wolf Point is located in the Fort Peck Indian Reservation.

Bottom: The staff at the Wolf Point Area Museum included Sarah Wagner (*left*) and Sandy Woodstock. Sarah grew up in this town of 2,700 and has made it her mission to explore the history of the town and its people. Sandy recently moved to town when her husband was assigned as minister of West Point Community Bible Church. She decided that volunteering at the museum would help her learn about her new home.

According to Sarah, it wasn't easy growing up in Wolf Point, a town of 2,700 in the middle of the Fort Peck Indian Reservation. "I've been to California and New Orleans, but moved back here because this is home."

Despite its northern location, Wolf Point sees wild swings in temperature, with summer temps as high as 110° F (43°C) and winter lows that dip down to −60°F (−51°C) with windchill.

"I have a friend in Iceland, and we figured that it actually gets colder here than where she lives," Sarah laughed.

Glad we came through in June!

NEXT STOP: JURASSIC LAKE

I had a package to mail, so we located a post office off U.S. Route 2. As I paid for the postage, the man behind the counter inquired about the graphics on our Bronco and Airstream. I explained that we were touring two-lane America. He suggested we visit Fort Peck Lake, 13 miles (21 kilometers) down the road.

"It's beautiful," he enthused. "The third largest earthen dam in the world: when the lake's full of water, its shoreline is longer than the California coastline."

We followed his advice, and the scene was indeed staggering. The lake is huge and beautiful, though it wasn't full when we visited. Seemingly another casualty of global warming, climate change, droughts, and so on.

Some interesting facts about Fort Peck Lake:

- Primary inflow: Missouri River
- Length at full pond: 134 miles (216 kilometers)
- Average depth: 76.3 feet (23.3 meters)
- Maximum depth: 220 feet (67 meters)
- Water volume: 18,687,731 acre feet (22.774 square kilometers)

The Fort Peck Dam was built in the 1930s to enhance navigation on the Missouri River and to manage the depth of the river, keeping it an average of 9 feet (2.7 meters) from Sioux City, Iowa, to St. Louis, Missouri. The lake was featured in the film *Jurassic Park III*, though no velociraptors were present the day we visited.

WANTED: FARMER

We'd driven through thousands of miles of farmland since the start of our journey, from Florida through Alabama, Kansas, and certainly in Nebraska, South Dakota, North Dakota, and now Montana. Whenever we asked about livelihoods and industries in the communities we visited, we were always told that agriculture was at or near the top of the list. In all those miles, MAR and I had yet to talk to any farmers. We decided to rectify that in Montana.

We were in the middle of thousands of acres of farms and would often see tractors working fields far from the road, but how could we actually meet a farmer? We exited U.S. Route 2 and began running dirt roads in a search for one of those long farm driveways, which we figured would lead us to a farmer. Or it'd get us arrested for trespassing.

Eventually we saw a series of barns and a couple of parked pickup trucks. Even a couple of city boys knew a real farmer couldn't be far.

We struck gold: there standing next to a huge combine was father-and-son farming team Rocky and Myles Kittleson of Glasgow, Montana. They greeted us and were eager to educate us about their livelihoods.

"We farm about 600 acres, mostly wheat, peas, and lentils, and have about 500 head of cattle," said Rocky, a rugged sixty-seven-year-old. I asked Rocky what his real name was. He replied that it was, um, Rocky. I wisely withheld any Bullwinkle jokes.

"We live in a dry climate, and get around 12 inches (30.5 centimeters) of rain in a good year," he said. "Last year we could only cut a couple of hundred acres because it was so dry. Right now it looks pretty good, but we need to get some rain pretty soon."

Rocky inherited the farm from his father, but the land was originally homesteaded by his great-grandfather, who arrived in Montana from Scandinavia. Today Rocky farms the fields with his two sons.

Myles is thirty-one years old, and he's getting ready to take over the farm. "I went to college at Montana Tech in Butte to become a mechanical engineer, but life changed," he shrugged. "There's a science to farming these days," so Myles is applying his studies right here on the farm.

THE PERKULATOR

HWY 2 E. POPLAR, MT 59255

The Perkulator was the most surprising coffee stop of all. Owned by two sisters, this quirky drive-through is shaped like a percolator coffee pot. The friendly staff makes a quick stop here mandatory.

Left: I wanted to meet a real farmer, so we drove down a dirt road until we found one who fit the bill. At the Kittleson farm, the father-and-son farming team of Rocky (*left*) and Myles explained the many challenges they face daily: the unpredictability of rain; the cost of equipment, fuel, and fertilizer; and other issues that farmers the world over must handle. They never have an easy day and seldom a day off.

Above: The 600-acre Kittleson farm. When we visited in late May 2022, Myles told us they'd received a decent amount of rain that spring and hoped the favorable weather would continue into the summer.

"The smaller farms are moving out and the bigger farms are getting bigger," said Rocky, who admits that even though the life is tough, he doesn't know what else he would do.

"I work on a mission trip every winter in Mexico, and I've been to Hawaii. That's it."

I was curious about equipment cost. "It wasn't but a few years ago that you could buy a complete farm for the cost of a piece of equipment these days," he said. "A sprayer is $200,000 and a cheaper combine will cost $300,000 to $400,000. The cost of fuel has gone up astronomically, and the cost of fertilizer has basically doubled.

"We go through dry spells from time to time, like in the 1980s. We buy insurance to get us through the bad years, otherwise we'd all be out of business."

Most of the farm's harvest goes to the West Coast, and much of the wheat goes to Japan. Rocky's durum wheat, goes mostly to pasta factories in North Dakota.

A few days earlier I'd never heard of seed cleaning, but after meeting Mike Hagen at that race track in North Dakota, I now felt like I was an expert. "So who cleans your seed, Rocky?" I asked nonchalantly. Turns out that he does it himself, and he showed me his seed-cleaning equipment.

We wrapped up our visit and drove off down the long dirt road back toward Highway 2, trailing a dust cloud behind us. It was dry and I hoped, like Rocky and Myles, that a steady rain would come soon.

Meeting farmers on their own turf underscored how important rain is, and how easily many of us can take it for granted. For farmers like Rocky and Myles, it's a key ingredient to success that can't be bought or counted on.

CAN'T JUDGE A BOOK . . .

Malta, Montana, didn't look like a town I'd ever care to live in. It's old, dirty, and mostly out of business. Still it was our home for the evening as we set up at a tiny campground attached to a small hotel a couple of blocks from the main street. The nice lady at the campground suggested the Stockman Bar & Steakhouse for dinner—she promised the place "offered the best steaks in town."

We walked from one end of Malta to the other. On our stroll, we saw the defunct Ford dealership, which we learned is now a local farmer's hobby shop featuring his collection Ford flathead V-8–powered cars. At one time this dealership was one of four auto dealers in town. Now, there are none.

Walking through the town depressed me. I told MAR that, if I was born here, I'd have escaped at eighteen years old and never looked back.

Little did I then realize that Malta would become one of the most significant stops on our road trip.

We got to the restaurant and saddled up to the bar. This was an authentic cowboy saloon—slightly worn out, slightly out of date, and serving an endless flow of Bud Light. A few pool tables and a coin-operated jukebox completed the image.

As usual, MAR walked in with cameras hanging from his neck. He laid them on top of the bar, garnering more attention from the locals than if he'd plopped a pistol there. We were instantly pegged as outsiders.

We were a long way from Davidson, North Carolina. Hell, we were a long way from anywhere. There weren't horses tied up out front, instead well-worn pickup trucks stood in their place, rode hard and put up wet. These were work trucks, many with saddles in the bed and most with a long gun or two in the rear window rack.

MAR and I were talking to the bartender about life in Malta when Daren Johannesen, seated at the bar near us, butted in amiably and started answering some of our questions. Daren is a fifty-three-year-old whose weather-worn appearance—from spending a life on the prairie—makes him look older than his years.

"I own a ranch in Loring, and used to raise wheat, barley, and oats, but with so little rain, it's a tough life," he said. "Now I just raise cattle."

Daren left farming for a while and worked in the oil fields of Williston, North Dakota, where he drove a truck and serviced oil rigs in the field. He gave that up in 1996.

"I've been to Canada a couple of times, hauling seed, and to Oregon and Washington, but never had any desire to move away," Daren said. "I quit high school after my freshman year and started working. I've never been married and never had any children.

"Back in the 1980s, this town was hopping. There was live music at three bars along the main street," Daren said, but explained why the town's once vibrant economy was fading.

"There was a plant near town that processed the mineral used to produce asbestos, but they cleared out all the minerals and closed the plant. Hundreds of people moved away. And the Pegasus Gold Corporation closed after a years-long battle with the EPA about water pollution."

Daren noted that the area is heavily populated by the descendants of Norwegian settlers who left their Nordic homeland to start new lives. "My grandfather came here from Norway in 1915 to stake his land claim—640 acres. He married a Canadian woman and they started building a family. He'd bring his grain to a Canadian rail station because it was closer to his land.

"People ask why I still live here, but there's no place like home."

Daren left after enjoying a couple of Mountain Dew sodas, but not before MAR could shoot a portrait of him outside the bar.

After Daren's departure, MAR and I got after what were perhaps the best steaks in town, but certainly not the best steaks of the trip. We struck up a conversation with another, much younger, cowboy. As it turned out, he was Daren's nephew.

Austin Wiese is twenty-five and must be the busiest cowboy in town. He's a full-time truck driver, a college student studying agriculture, and he farms a piece of land.

"Farming is just not sustainable," Austin recounted. "Between the land I own and what I lease, I've got 3,000 acres. Last year I had a grasshopper infestation. If I hire a crop-duster, it'll cost $11–$14 an acre to kill those grasshoppers. It'll take two or three days, but it'll cost me $42,000."

Most farmers lost their hay crop because they couldn't afford the crop-dusting.

"What some of us started to do is spray only the circumference of our fields and cross our fingers that the critters wouldn't get into the interior," he said.

Top left: This billboard took the words right out of my mouth. With a population of 3,202 residents, Glasgow is the twenty-third largest city in Montana and the largest population hub for more than 100 miles (160 kilometers) in any direction. Which makes it precisely the middle of nowhere.

Top right: The nice woman who runs this campground told us the best food in Malta was at the Stockman Bar & Steakhouse. MAR and I toured the town, and I was not impressed. In fact, Malta was my least favorite town of our trip to that point. Twenty-four hours later, my opinion had taken a 180-degree turn.

Opposite: The first cowboy we met was Daren Johannesen, a lifetime rancher and truck driver. He was born in Malta and quit school after ninth grade to go farming. His Chevy pickup parked outside Stockman's would have been a horse 100 years ago. Daren's grandfather moved to Montana from Norway and homesteaded the same 640 acres (2.6 square kilometers) the family farms today.

WE WERE A LONG WAY FROM DAVIDSON,
NORTH CAROLINA. HELL, WE WERE A LONG
WAY FROM ANYWHERE.

Left: After Daren Johannesen went out, his nephew, Austin Wiese, sat down on the same barstool and picked up where his uncle had left off. Austin, also a farmer, told us the problems he faces with grasshoppers eating his crops. The hat Austin is wearing was purchased for $20 by his grandfather in a Malta clothing store some sixty years ago.

Opposite, top: I was part of a cattle drive and met Steven's neighbors, friends, and a few high school students, the latter group volunteering when a farmer needs help with branding his cattle. When I woke up that morning I never thought I'd spend the day riding a horse and participating in cattle roundup.

Opposite, bottom: In just a few minutes, high school students perform several procedures on calves that wouldn't make them popular in singles bar.

Buying hay to replace the lost crop is an expensive proposition. Two years ago, quality hay cost $115 per ton; in 2022, even the cheap hay cost $400 per ton.

"It's called survival, just trying to make it through to the next year, when we hope things'll get better," he lamented.

Austin wore what was apparently a high-quality, non-cowboy hat. It was certainly a Western-style hat, but more like something a barroom piano player might wear while banging away on the keys as fistfights broke around him.

"My grandfather bought this hat in the early 1960s from that store on the corner," he said, pointing to the clothing shop across the street. "He paid $20 for it, and it's still in great condition after almost sixty years."

It was getting late and Austin excused himself. He drove off in his pickup, a busy young man with a lot of responsibility on his shoulders.

SEEING A MAN ABOUT A HORSE

Next a tall fellow who'd been playing pool in the next room came over and introduced himself. He was Steven Johannesen, also Daren's nephew. "Before my uncle left, he told me you guys want to learn about life out here."

"Our farm's about 50 miles north of here. If you'll meet me at 7 a.m. tomorrow morning, I'll show you what life is really like in northern Montana," he promised.

What an amazing offer from a stranger. We were in.

The next morning, my opinion of Malta changed.

We met Steven at his family's ranch, about 2 miles (3 kilometers) south of the Canadian border. "That's your horse over there," he said.

"Steven, I don't ride horses," I noted.

"You do now," he said, guiding my foot into the stirrup and my body into the saddle.

"THE PEOPLE YOU MET TODAY ARE THE NICEST, HARDEST-ASS PEOPLE YOU'LL EVER MEET IN YOUR LIFE."

"This is Savage, but don't let the name scare you," Steven said of my thirteen-year-old steed. "He is my daughter's horse, and he's gentle."

I was part of a cattle drive, and totally out of my element. I had last ridden a horse when I was about twelve. Now, I was a rider on branding day, an exercise where calves and their mommas are rounded up and penned.

I'm sure there were some chuckles going on behind my back: I was surrounded by a bunch of real cowboys *looking like real cowboys*—boots, denim, cowboy hats—and here I was wearing my favorite college basketball team sweatshirt, *Barn Find Hunter* hat, and Top-Sider boat shoes.

I was one of about a dozen cowboys on horseback. We were aided by six more on four-wheelers, a mechanical version of a horse that, I was told, only need to be "fed" when they're used.

Probably the hardest-working cattle wranglers were the herding dogs, who quickly chased down and returned scared calves intent on escaping to the hills. These smart and energetic dogs have an admirable work ethic.

Steven told me that cattle farmers prefer to brand calves when they're one week to two months old, otherwise they become too large to wrestle.

Savage took off in a trot—certainly not at my behest—and I realized I had no idea how to put on the brakes. Thankfully Savage realized that the idiot on his back was literally along for the ride. Rather than collide with a bunch of other horses, he applied his own brakes. Sort of an equestrian version of a self-driving car.

Seeing my unnecessary distress, Steven informed me that the rider should pull back on the reigns to slow or stop the horse. Noted.

What happens if one of the cows wanders off to Canada? "It happens occasionally," Steven admitted. "I can't chase it because there are sensors that will detect someone trying to jump over the border. So I'll call one of my Canadian farmer friends and ask if they can find the cow. Then we'll meet at the border crossing, and he'll hand it over. The border guards don't give us a hard time."

After all the cows and calves were contained in a portable pen, the process of separating the angry momma cows from their frightened calves began. This involved twenty cowboys, a handful of youngsters, and those hard-working dogs. It's a kind of chaotic ballet, chasing the 2,000-pound cows outside the pen with small flags and noisemakers on long sticks, then roping the babies with lassos. A cacophony of frantic mooing rises to deafening levels as the calves are dragged by horse to another area, where boys and girls from the local high school wrestle the calves to the ground.

Once down, the calves undergo a three-minute procedure. First a colored tag is inserted into one ear. Then they're injected with a vaccine to protect them from a bovine version of Covid.

The next part got me a little squeamish: after the comparatively minor tagging and vaccination, the boy calves are castrated. This was accomplished with a scissor-looking device that resembled a tree pruner. Ouch. (One of the high school girls seemed particularly skilled at this procedure. Tread carefully, young cowboys!) Steven told me that, when done correctly, neutering calves is completely bloodless.

Lastly the calf is branded. A hot iron with the farm's distinct logo is held to the calf's hindquarters, and the animal commences to mooing bloody murder. I found this upsetting, but I was assured by one of the cowboys that the calves are screaming because they're scared. "Their skin is so thick they hardly feel it."

Still, for a city boy, a rather harrowing experience as the smell of burning flesh and hair filled the air.

Steven told me that all the people helping out were local farmers and farm hands. "They're our friends and neighbors. We'll all get together at one farm and help that farmer brand his calves one day, then two days later we'll all meet at another farm and help that family."

Steven was a cowboy, no doubt, but the divorced father of two seemed somehow different from his neighbors, in part because he had a college degree and had lived in Chicago for a spell.

Gazing at the wide-open country, I had to wonder: how does a single guy meet a woman when you're 50 miles (80 kilometers) from even a small town?

"The internet," he said matter-of-factly. I don't know why I thought the answer would be any different. "I have a girlfriend in Glasgow, 100 miles away."

Not surprisingly, the internet and Amazon have changed the lives of rural farmers, drawing them closer to the rest of the world, if only virtually.

Twenty-four hours before this moment, I'd told MAR that I would hate to live in a place like Malta, but that's because I had judged a book by its cover. It seemed a dirty, worn-down town in need of a fresh coat of paint on virtually every surface. And I hadn't even met anyone who lived there. Still I wondered what kept a guy like Steven there?

Above: Freshly minted campground owners Dave and Cheree Waddell and their daughter Damaka. Dave was laid off from a corporate job in Oregon because of the pandemic, so the family hit the road in a camper, eventually deciding to become campground owners in rural Shelby, Montana. Except for the bitterly cold winters, the family loves their new lifestyle.

"I wanted to be an underwater welder, so I went to college to learn auto mechanics, then to learn welding," he explained. "But my grandfather came here from Norway over 100 years ago. I'm the fourth generation to farm this land.

"How could I leave this place? I love it here."

As MAR and I walked toward our Bronco/Airstream rig, which was parked among a couple dozen large pickup trucks, we said good-bye to some of the cowboys we had met that morning. One young guy walked over to tell me that he regularly watched *Barn Find Hunter*.

Then he said something that truly registered with me, having spent my morning riding with a bunch of cowboys: "The people you met today are the nicest, hardest-ass people you'll ever meet in your life."

No doubt.

When I ran a public relations agency, I constantly reminded my staff that every person you meet has an interesting story inside them and that it only takes a little digging to uncover it. A guy in a cowboy hat and about 500 head of cattle brought that lesson home to me.

A PANDEMIC POSITIVE

Back to Malta, 50 miles (80 kilometers) south, and we were again westbound on Highway 2. We needed a place spend the night and decided that the Lewis & Clark RV Park in Shelby looked good, at least online.

Shelby, Montana, is a town of about 3,200. It was founded in 1892 and named after Peter O. Shelby, general manager of the Montana Central Railway. In an effort to promote Shelby, city fathers organized the World Heavyweight Championship fight between Jack Dempsey and Tommy Gibbons on July 4, 1923. This being during the Great Depression, local folks could not afford admission, and only 8,000 tickets were sold. Just before the fight, though, 4,000 farmers stormed the gates and saw the fight for free. The two boxers went 15 rounds, with Dempsey called the winner over Gibbons, but the episode almost bankrupt the town.

Shelby is home to a steakhouse that came highly recommended, which was reason enough to bunk there for the night. Oddly, though, the menu offered only one cut, a ribeye. Sure, it was a pretty good steak, but only one option in a Montana steakhouse?

Back at the campground, MAR and I gabbed with the owners while checking in. Dave and Cheree Waddell had only owned the campground since 2020. And campground ownership had not been in the couple's long-term plans.

"We had a nice life in central Oregon," said forty-eight-year-old Dave. "I'd worked for five years in the aerospace industry as a quality supervisor. Then at the end of March 2020 we were all laid off because of the Covid pandemic. It was only supposed to be for two weeks."

But two weeks led to four, which lead to eight. Dave filed for unemployment. Then he got word that he wouldn't be called back in 2020.

"We had our savings, so I wasn't really worried," Dave explained. "We decided to spend some time on a road trip, so we bought a Class C motorhome and hit the road to Montana, South Dakota, North Dakota, and Wyoming."

The Waddells had visited Yellowstone in the past, but they'd never been to Mount Rushmore or the Badlands. During that extended camping adventure, Dave had a brainstorm about a new direction for their lives.

"Hey, Honey, what do you think about owning a campground?'" I asked Cheree. "It started out as a joke, but once I decided that I wasn't going to wait around to be called back to work, we got more serious about the idea."

The Waddells began learning about campgrounds and searched the internet for campgrounds that were for sale. They looked in Wyoming, Idaho, and Montana before finally settling on the Lewis & Clark RV Park in Shelby, a 9-acre park with space for sixty campers.

"An eighty-six-year-old man owned the place, and he was physically unable to maintain the grounds because he was on oxygen," said Dave. "And he was extremely rude to the guests, threatening to shoot their dogs, turning off the Wi-Fi, criticizing campers for using too much water."

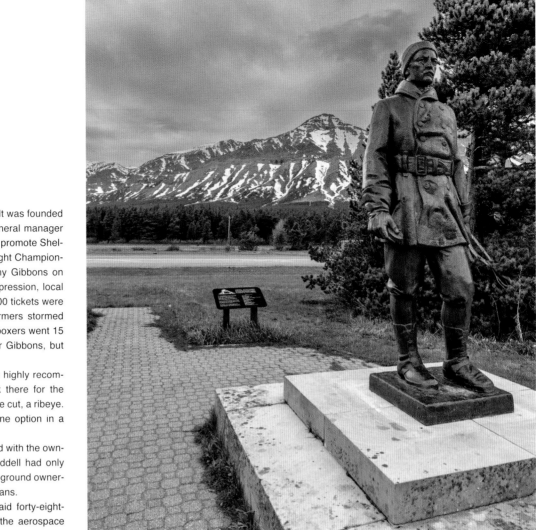

It was so bad that people in town wouldn't recommend the campground to tourists.

With summertime temperatures in the 90s and winter temps as low as −45°F—plus windchills down to −65°F—Cheree wasn't so sure about the family's move.

"In the beginning it was a challenge," she recalled. "I was crying every day. But now it's awesome. The people here are great."

Dave and Cheree's thirteen-year-old daughter, Damaka, has special needs, and they were initially concerned about the area schools, but found them excellent. We met Damaka as well. She was precious and beautiful, and both MAR and I instantly fell in love with her.

In the two years the Waddells have owned the business, its reputation has improved. Word has gotten out about the new ownership, and people in town recommend the campground again.

A rare happy ending to a story that started with a pandemic layoff.

Above: As we approached the Rocky Mountains, we stopped to inspect this monument to Theodore Roosevelt, who was instrumental in making conservation a national priority.

Top: These Rocky Mountain peaks were visible from the east about 100 miles (160 kilometers) away. They were our first sign that we were approaching Glacier National Park, its 1-million acres (4,050 square kilometers) stretching to the Canadian border. It was June, but the Going-to-the-Sun Road was still not open for the season, so we had to drive around the southern end of the park.

Bottom: The Isaacsons were also staying at the amazing KOA campground at the park's western entrance. They met in Alaska fifty-five years ago, when Ike was working on a Dalton Highway road crew from Fairbanks to Deadhorse. I peppered him with questions about the legendary road we would soon travel.

WELCOME TO WALLER FORD

Leaving Shelby, MAR took the morning drive shift and I worked on my notes in the passenger seat. As we crested a rise in the road, I looked up and saw snow-covered peaks.

"My goodness," I said to MAR. "There it is: Glacier National Park!"

People from North Dakota on had told us that snow-covered peaks would suddenly appear when we were about 50 miles (80 kilometers) from the park's eastern entrance. I'd been looking forward to driving through the park on Going-to-the-Sun-Road.

About an hour east of the park, we passed through the town of Cut Bank. After fueling up at what MAR deemed an acceptable coffee shop, I noticed a Ford dealership with a four-door Bronco similar to ours on display. "We should make their day and pull into that dealership for a few minutes," I suggested. "I'm sure they'll get a kick out of it."

We made a U-turn and pulled into the small, crowded parking lot.

The showroom and offices emptied quickly as employees took out their cellphones, began snapping selfies in front of our lettered-up Bronco, and peppering us with questions.

"Where are you going? When will you get there? What are you doing here?"

Eventually we met General Manager Josh Waller, whose father bought the dealership in 1978. Having worked in a Ford dealership on Long Island forty years ago, I also had some questions.

"How many salesmen? How many new cars do you move a year? Whose miniature Mustang is that out there?"

Josh explained that the dealership had three salesmen, and that in a typical year they sold about 115 new cars. "We're in the middle of nowhere. We're over 100 miles from the closest Walmart and 47 miles to the next Ford dealership. All the new cars I have coming in were sold months ago.

"Every summer we'd sell new cars to tourists coming through town whose cars would have some terminal problem, even blown engines. There aren't enough new cars to sell these days, but we're selling lots of nice used cars."

As for the miniature Mustang, Josh said, "That's a go-kart with a gas engine. My dad bought it about fifteen years ago. I drove it to work today."

You drove a *go-kart* to work?

"I only live a few blocks away, and I know all the policemen around here anyway," he said.

To demonstrate his point, he pulled the cord to fire up the engine and cut a few laps around the parking lot.

The Waller Ford employees still outside shook their heads at the sight. It was common knowledge that Josh did goofy things once in a while—a benefit of being the boss.

Left: John Waller bought the Ford dealership in Cut Bank, Montana, in 1978, and has since turned over the management to his sons Josh, currently the general manager, and Matt. Josh drives to work from his home a few blocks away in this gas-powered 1967 Ford Mustang go-kart.

Above: Because the middle section of the Going-to-the-Sun Road was closed, the drive could only be accessed from either the east or the west side of the park. We drove the Bronco, sans Airstream, a few miles from the western entrance before we had to make a U-turn. We were treated to this pleasant location along the route.

KOA DELUXE

Glacier National Park had campgrounds within the park's boundaries, but because we were usually LIFO—last-in, first-out—we didn't feel it would be neighborly to our fellow campers to disrupt their sleep with our setting up or breaking down camp while they slumbered.

We ended up at the mother of all KOA campgrounds, the best I've ever visited: West Glacier KOA Resort. It looked brand-spanking new. I can't imagine the kind of investment required to buy this property and build a facility like this. It would be our home only for a night, but I could certainly see how campers might want to spend a week here.

The registration building doubled as a general store. There was an onsite restaurant (pro tip: don't order the ribs), along with an onsite coffee shop and ice cream parlor. Hmm, maybe we *should* stay for a week. The pool seemed more like something you'd find at an upscale resort. In the evening, there were organized seminars, free for campers to attend. The evening we stayed, local naturalists offered a lecture about birds of prey.

As always, fellow travelers were curious about the Airstream Basecamp 16X we towed behind our Bronco. Mer-rilee Isaacson, from North Bend, Washington, was one of the curious campers.

She and her husband, Ike, traveled in a van-based Class B motorhome. They had traded in a Mercedes-Benz Sprinter for their new Dodge Ram rig.

The Isaacsons had been married for fifty-five years. Ike suffered from congestive heart failure, but the couple had never lost their wanderlust.

"We met in 1966 when I was sixteen years old," said Merrilee. "My folks ran a lodge in Alaska, and I worked there in the summer. We were married the next summer.

"Ike had a heart attack twenty-two years ago, then soon had another one," she went on. Ike had qualified for a heart transplant, but Alaska didn't have a medical facility that could perform the procedure, so they moved to Washington and bought a house next to a fire station so they would be near trained paramedics and an ambulance.

"He waited nineteen months, but eventually a heart was identified when a young man in Spokane died in an accident in 2000," Merilee explained. "Our daughter was scheduled to be married around that time, but she moved the wedding to 6 a.m. on the day of Ike's transplant right in Ike's hospital room because she wanted her father to be there."

"VWS ARE ALL I'VE DRIVEN SINCE I WAS SIXTEEN YEARS OLD, WHICH IS UNUSUAL BECAUSE I WEIGH 300 POUNDS AND I PLAY THE TUBA."

"Once I got the new heart, I felt like a new person," Ike enthused. "I had no more chest pain." The couple has been traveling nonstop since.

Ike spent much of his working life as an employee of Alaska's Department of Transportation. He drove road graders on many of the roads we would be traveling in the coming weeks, especially the Dalton Highway, the sole land route from Fairbanks to Deadhorse.

Eventually Ike left Alaska's DOT to work on the Trans-Alaska Pipeline System.

"We usually take three major camping trips each year," said Merrilee. "We've been to the Redwoods, Michigan, the ocean, Colorado. We just really enjoy getting out."

NOT GOING-TO-THE-SUN ROAD

One of the most popular attractions in Glacier National Park is Going-to-the-Sun Road, an east-west route that passes through some of the park's most spectacular features over a 50-mile (80-kilometer) stretch. I have friends who've taken part in the annual Going to the Sun Vintage Car Rally, so I'd been looking forward to checking out the road myself. Because some of the turns are tight, we decided to disconnect the Airstream and leave it at the campground.

A complete trek wasn't in the cards, though, as we learned that much of the road was closed due to snow and road construction—it was accessible for only a few miles from either the east or west park entrances. We managed only 10 miles (16 kilometers) before we had to turn around and cover our tracks on the same road. So much for photo opportunities.

LONG-HAUL HERBIE

We were filling up the Bronco and buying some huckleberry pie (a local delicacy) when a vintage VW Beetle tooled past us.

"Michael, look at that!" I called out excitedly. "That's an early one: a pre-1967." As a longtime VW enthusiast, I could tell the car's era by its early chrome bumpers and traditional nonvertical Beetle headlights.

But what really made this VW stand out was its "Herbie, the Love Bug" paint scheme and graphics.

As luck would have it—and because our Bronco traveled faster than the Herbie Beetle—we had the VW in our sights an hour or so after our fuel stop.

I was determined to catch that car, which was a challenging feat on two-lane Highway 2. It required some trick passing maneuvers, but I gradually reeled in the little car.

I wanted to flag the driver to pull over. I had no idea if the driver would comprehend my wild gestures at 60 miles per hour (97 kilometers per hour) or instead think he was being carjacked.

I pulled to the VW's right, the Bronco's right-side tires on the dirt shoulder (don't tell Ford), and rolled down the window. The driver waved and gave me a thumbs up, perhaps hoping that I would simply go away. But eventually I was able to holler to him that I would like to have a chat.

He understood and pulled into a parking lot. I guess I don't look like a complete psychotic. He was followed by a late-model Jeep Wrangler, which also pulled into the lot.

The driver jumped out of the VW and introduced himself as Clayton Capps, along with his mother and codriver, Veda Capps.

Below: Clayton lives a full life. Before this trip with his mother, he drove the same VW from Texas to Daytona Beach, Florida, for a car show, then three weeks later drove it to Wisconsin for a Polka festival. The 1963 Beetle is Clayton's daily driver and has more than 1 million miles (1,600,000 kilometers) on the body and almost 200,000 miles (322,000 kilometers) on the engine.

"We left home in Salado, Texas, and have so far visited New Mexico, Yellowstone, Wyoming, and Glacier National Park," Clayton said. "From here we're heading toward the Olympic Peninsula in Washington, then down the California Coast, the San Diego Zoo, Mojave Desert, Las Vegas, and the Grand Canyon before we get back home to Texas—probably seventeen, eighteen, nineteen days altogether."

Wait, what?

This was very much a vintage car, nearly sixty years old. Only crazy people take long trips in old cars. People like me. I needed to learn more.

"My husband doesn't like to go anywhere," shrugged Veda. "He's back home in Salado."

Clayton confided in me that his mom almost didn't come because she felt obligated to stay home with his dad. But after he installed air conditioning in the Beetle for her, she agreed to come along.

Air conditioning in a 40-horsepower Beetle?

"This is my daily driver," he said. "I bought it from the original owner in 2005."

Clayton had modified the VW for long-distance driving, including installing a larger, 1,600cc engine.

"The engine is a Mexican-built model, and it has 196,000 miles on it," he said. I was floored, but it explained how the car was able to speed along despite having air conditioning.

"And the body and chassis have 1,071,352 miles on them."

This was amazing. I'm a lifelong VW guy, but the mileage numbers were outrageous. Clayton owns twenty-five VWs, including one of the eleven Beetles that Disney Productions used in the Herbie/Love Bug movies. This explained a lot.

"That Beetle was nicknamed Junkie, it was parked in the back of the Disney lot after filming," he said.

"VWs are all I've driven since I was sixteen years old, which is unusual because I weigh 300 pounds and I play the tuba."

Clayton had begun planning his trip in December 2021. He and his friend Gary Schiller performed a number of maintenance chores on the Beetle, specifically rebuilding the steering box, refreshing the engine, installing new rear seals, repacking the wheel bearings, adjusting the brakes, and greasing the torque tube.

"I have all the tools and parts I'd need if I get into trouble," Clayton said. This is why his friend Gary was following in the Jeep. Clayton's VW was packed to the headliner with camping gear, clothing, tools, and parts. Additional items were in

Above: We first saw this "Herbie" VW while gassing up near Glacier National Park. Several hours later, we finally caught up with the car and convinced the driver to pull over. Clayton Capps and his eighty-five-year-old mother, Veda, had left Texas several days earlier en route to explore the northwestern United States.

Above: Clayton had planned to ship the VW to Europe in 2020 before Covid ended those plans. Hearing we were on our way to Alaska, he admitted the forty-ninth state is on his bucket list. Even though Clayton weighs 300 pounds (136 kilograms) and his mother is riding shotgun, the tiny VW has enough room for camping gear, clothes, tools, and spares. A true road-tripper.

the support vehicle, along with Gary's wife Desiré and his daughters Kylie and Autumn, eight years and one year old respectively. Despite its burden, the VW had managed 24 to 33 miles per gallon (10 to 14 kilometers per liter), depending on elevation and headwinds.

Each day at about 5 p.m., they decide where they'll spend the night and whether it will be in a tent or a hotel.

Clearly this was not Clayton's first long trip in his Beetle. He'd recently driven the same VW from Salado to Daytona Beach, Florida, for a car show, then headed to Wisconsin for a polka festival—with his tuba. And he confided that a trip to Alaska was on his bucket list.

Clearly Clayton Capps subscribes to the Hagerty slogan: Never Stop Driving.

THE PALE (ALE) RIDER

At lunchtime we approached Libby, Montana. We picked Cabinet Mountain Brewing based on its online reviews.

We didn't know about consuming a beer with lunch, but I felt a need for roughage: salad, vegetables, and the like. And what goes best with roughage? Beer. Decision made.

I ordered the Last Best Pale Ale. Perfect. You see, I have this theory when it comes to microbreweries: many of them make sours, fruity concoctions, stouts, too many IPAs, and Lord knows what other varieties, but few can make a quality pale ale, the most standard of brews. So that's what I order, at least as my first beer. It allows me to judge the quality of the brewery's products and the probable quality of their other offerings.

The Last Best Pale Ale was excellent, as was their food. Theory proven once again.

After lunch we hit our old friend Highway 2 and continued our westward trek. Montana is a *huge* state, and we'd spent six days traversing it. It's also a geographically diverse state. A few days before we had rolled over some of the flattest land we'd seen on our entire tour up to that point. But headed toward the state's western boundary, we experienced an entirely different character, moving from barren to richly nourished, from flat to mountainous.

I knew that south of our route were all the billionaire ranches and their amazing vintage cars, but I'm glad we decided to travel the northern route and experience real sights and real people.

5.
NORTHWEST PASSAGE

LIVING THROUGH THE SEATTLE FREEZE

Welcome to Idaho, where the roads become instantly rough!

We are 4,811 miles (7,743 kilometers) into our road trip and entering the second-to-last state on the first leg of this journey.

Before we departed, I checked the mileage from Key West to Seattle using MapQuest. It calculated about 3,500 miles (5,633 kilometers), but that would have been following interstate highways. Our goal, though, has always been to avoid interstates at all cost and to travel this great country on two-lane roads.

Our mileage increased when we decided to add North Dakota to our route. Taking the road less travelled can have its downsides. Thankfully, we have no agenda. The ideal road trip should put a premium on the experience, with no time constraints.

Whenever possible, take the long way.

According to the map, we wouldn't be in Idaho long because we were way up north, where the state narrows to just 50 miles (80 kilometers) wide.

I'd never been this far north in the state. I had spent time here about fifteen years before while hosting a media event for Mercedes-Benz where they launched the then new GL-Class SUV. The event was based in McCall, Idaho, a beautiful part of the state inhabited by the billionaires who had run out Sun Valley's millionaires. Whatever—it was beautiful.

While my team scouted the state for driving routes, restaurants, and scenic bathroom breaks, I brought my elderly mother along to experience a part of the United States she had never seen. Mom had recently lost her husband, my stepfather, and was feeling down, so I felt a week of driving around Idaho was in order. My mother, who was born in Germany and had escaped to America during World War II, had lived her entire life on Long Island. Her idea of an interesting trip did not include Idaho.

"Tommy, I never thought I'd visit Idaho," she remarked at the time. "It is one of the most beautiful places I have ever been."

I couldn't agree more.

HIPPIE COMMERCE

I'm old enough to have been a hippie, but I escaped that fate. Oh, I had long hair back in the day, but in my teens and early twenties I identified more with surfers. And gearheads, needless to say. While my friends were at Woodstock or doing drugs, I was either rebuilding a carburetor or trying to remain upright on a surfboard.

Hippie or not, when we saw the Loveworks Hippie Store in Ponderay, Idaho, we had to stop. A hippie store selling tie-dyed shirts, tapestries, and jewelry in 2022? Couldn't be.

But it was.

Self-described Jesus freaks Michael and Tina Puckett started selling apparel out of their 1963 International Harvester bus nearly forty years ago. When the couple started a family, a second floor was added to the bus.

"The bus is called Ruack, which translates to, 'the wind blows where it pleases,'" explained sixty-five-year-old

Bottom left: "This is the dawning of the age of Aquarius. . . ." How could we not stop? The Loveworks Hippie Store reminded me of Woodstock, Jimi Hendrix, and head shops all wrapped in one! Michael and Tina Puckett and their family have been making and selling tie-dyed shirts since 1987, much of the time from out of the two-story bus in the background, as they traveled around the United States. More recently they've worked from this retail location in Ponderay, Idaho.

Bottom right: Michael and Tina, along with their some of their seven children, manufacture and sell tie-dyed shirts. All their kids grew up in their 1963 International school bus, which pulled a VW Microbus behind it. Today the bus serves as a billboard to attract attention to their retail store. It certainly worked for us!

Michael. "We began making tie-dye shirts and selling them out of the bus in 1984. We traveled the country until six or seven years ago. We caught the tail end of the hippie movement. We sell the whole hippie experience, but we're not a drug paraphernalia store.

"We were running restaurants, but decided to drop out of the rat race. Living in a bus may sound glamorous, but when it breaks down on the side of the road and you have no money to repair it, you need to put your faith in God. We always made it."

Michael is a big man with long blonde hair and a powerful voice. He projects a gentle side as he recites Bible verses, but he has another side as well: though probably not unusual for Idaho, he told me he always carries a loaded pistol.

That's all I will say on that subject.

The Pucketts' seven children all grew up in the bus. When they set up their mobile store on the main street or along the Interstate, the children became the show. Today the family has a proper house adjacent to the store, and the bus is a lawn ornament for the business. Half the kids are out of the house, while the smaller kids are still around.

Michael said business is brisk. Besides the Idaho location, he has another on the coast in Lincoln City, Oregon, which is open 24/7. "That store does five times as much business as we do. Like $3,000 per day.

"Tie-dye is about color, and color makes people happy. And these days, people just want to be happy."

RAIN AND FLOWERS IN WASHINGTON

The moment we entered Washington, the sky opened up and it has been pouring rain nearly all day! MAR nailed it precisely: "Perfect, we enter Washington and it begins to rain. Isn't that the way it's supposed to be?"

The rain finally stopped after about three hours, and the colors in the sky were fabulous, with bright sun near and threatening skies in the distance.

Approaching a huge field of sun-yellow flowers, I told MAR we needed to pull over and shoot our travel rig against that background.

The next hour or so was devoted to shooting stills, plus videos from the drone. As the sky transitioned from dark to light and from storm to sun, all played against the yellow flowers, it was an hour well spent.

But daylight was running down, and we still had over two hours of travel time to reach our campsite in Winthrop. We had made reservations a few hours earlier, but at that point we'd been overly optimistic. We were both getting dozy, but I was eager to see Winthrop for the first time in probably twenty-five years. I had vacationed then with my wife and young son in the Cascade Mountains at a resort called the Sun Mountain Lodge. It was a great week, so when I discovered that there was a KOA campground in Winthrop, I was eager to see the town again.

But that was not to be. We were beat, it had started to rain again (imagine that), and it was getting late.

DAM AMAZING

The Grand Coulee Dam is an amazing piece of engineering. Constructed over a nine-year period, from 1933 to 1942, it towers 550 feet (168 meters) above the Columbia River. Though the Hoover Dam gets all the love, Grand Coulee Dam is the largest power-generating station in the United States. Two lakes lie behind it: Franklin Delano Roosevelt Lake and Banks Lake. We drove around the latter.

The dam is one of the largest structures in the world, containing nearly 12 million cubic yards (9,174,658 cubic meters) of concrete, enough to build a sidewalk 4 feet (1.2 meters) wide, 4 inches (10 centimeters) thick, twice around the globe at the equator!

As the dam was nearing completion in 1941, a documentary film captured its progress and promise. Woody Guthrie, who had recently moved to the area with his family in search of a job, was approached by the film's director about writing music and narrating the film. In an epic example of over-delivering, he wrote twenty-six songs, including "Roll On Columbia, Roll On" and "Grand Coulee Dam." The film was finally completed in 1949, having been put on hold during World War II.

Besides the sheer volume of energy it was capable of producing, the Grand Coulee Dam offers a recreational paradise for fishermen, power boaters, and adventurers. There's even a laser light show that projects life-size images of battleships and the Statue of Liberty on the dam during the summer months.

BEST CAMPGROUND BY A DAM SITE

We decided to forgo our fancy $75 campsite, instead opting for a "replacement" campsite near the Grand Coulee Dam that was slightly rough around the edges but would suffice for the evening. We ate dinner at the campground's restaurant and sat at the bar next to a drunk patron, who I believe was actually an off-duty employee. This dude started coughing and couldn't stop. If he was ill with Covid-19 or TB or something else, MAR and I were sure to catch it. After about his tenth major coughing attack, MAR got up and left the room.

When we broke camp the next morning, we drove on roads that skirted the Grand Coulee Dam. That might have been our best driving decision of the entire trip so far.

Here we'd driven more than 5,000 miles (8,047 kilometers) from Key West and had stumbled upon some of the most beautiful scenery we'd seen. The landscape—mountains, dam, lake, and river—were almost too much to comprehend on that foggy, drizzly morning.

Left: We spent the night at a campground near the Grand Coulee Dam. Neither of us had any real knowledge of the area. When we woke up the next morning, its beauty captivated us: we were in midst of a miniature Grand Canyon with majestic cliffs and a deep valley carved out over millions of years by the Columbia River.

Right: A vintage photo of one of the most ambitious concrete engineering projects ever tackled: Washignton's Grand Coulee Dam. Constructed between 1933 and 1942, it held back the Columbia River in Washington with nearly 12 million cubic yards of concrete in order to produce hydroelectric power.

Left: MAR must have special powers, because the first business we passed after exiting the Grand Coulee Dam that cold, damp morning was Banks Lake Brew & Bistro. Named for the reservoir formed by the Columbia River, Michelle Winteroth (left) and Cori Tipps were a sight for sore eyes as they served us two weary campers proper cups of joe and homemade pastries.

Below: We were in the right place at the right time, invited to display our rig at the Avants Classics on the Green in Woodinville. The show was a little gem, casual, with none of the high-pressure judging I'm used from similar events in Pebble Beach and Amelia Island.

"IN SEATTLE, YOU HAVEN'T HAD ENOUGH COFFEE UNTIL YOU CAN THREAD A SEWING MACHINE WHILE IT'S RUNNING." — JEFF BEZOS

CONCOURS DE CRUD

As we approached Seattle and the end of our journey's first leg, real life began to intrude. No longer were we out of cellphone range, camping out on the prairie. We faced flights back home in a few days: MAR to Northern California, me to Maine. We decided early on that the only way we could fit this eight-week roadtrip into our otherwise busy lives would require a mid-adventure pit stop, a sort of intermission in order to take care photography clients (MAR) and film *Barn Find Hunter* episodes (me), plus catch up on a long list of Honey-Dos. But until then, we had more people to meet and more coffee to drink.

One of MAR's friends, Curtis Creager, a fellow car enthusiast and photographer, had been following our adventure on Instagram. He had an intriguing invitation.

"You know, there's an event tomorrow, Concours at the Vineyard, and I think I can get you guys in."

He didn't mean free admission: he meant that we might be able to display the Bronco and Airstream rig on the show field. We were all for it, as long as we could display our filthy vehicles in their natural state.

Permission arrived and we rolled onto the field among a bevy of classic cars.

For the next few hours, MAR and I played the role of product specialists for both the Bronco and the Airstream. We explained the features and answered questions about our book project.

It's funny, but *many* of the attendees, including entrants with very valuable cars, beat a path to our filth-encrusted rig—maybe *because* it was so filthy? More likely the Bronco and Airstream suggested adventure and a story in the way that no perfectly restored car ever can.

STEELHEAD TROUT WITH ORANGE CRUSH

After the Vineyard show, we headed south to the beautiful home of Cars Yeah Podcast host Mark Greene in Gig Harbor. MAR and I have each been guests on Mark's show, and earlier that day we thought it would be fun to contact Mark and offer to do a two-for-one in-person interview for his program. In discussing our idea, Mark noted that, of the thousands of shows he's recorded, none had ever been in person—all had been via Zoom.

"Sure, that would be fun," he said. "Come on over."

En route to his house, Mark called again, "Would you guys like to stay over, sleep in a real bed, and enjoy a home-cooked meal?"

Oh, do you mean rather than another dinner of peanut-butter-and-jelly sandwiches followed by a serenade of MAR's? We jumped at the offer and enjoyed a wonderful steelhead trout dinner and two cozy bedrooms.

We happened to be visiting as Mark was in the process of selling his beloved Porsche 911 on Bring a Trailer. The car is well known among Porsche enthusiasts. Nicknamed Orange Crush, it's one of three 930 Turbos featuring a special paint-to-sample build by the factory. It was a beautiful sight in Mark's garage. We decided that we would tape the podcast and watch the end of the auction before leaving the next morning.

That night heavy rain (Washington, right?) knocked out the power to the Mark's part of town, so not only could Mark not record the show, he also missed the end of his car's auction.

HEY, GET OFF MY LAWN!

Come morning, we bid Mark farewell and left Gig Harbor proceeding toward Issaquah, ready to find a coffee shop (of course). The plan was to sit down with our brew of choice and peruse maps of the area for likely places to do some barn find hunting before we headed home.

You expect to find good coffee shops in Seattle, but we had help locating the best ones thanks to MAR's friends, Ant Matsuda and Toni Pinto, who live in Issaquah, near the city.

BANKS LAKE BREW & BISTRO

9701 U.S. ROUTE 2, COULEE CITY, WA 99115

Banks Lake Brew & Bistro is an early-morning stop like no other. The fresh-made pastries and breakfast treats along with great coffee will get your day started right. Ignore the fact that it's attached to a gas station.

When he got in touch with them, they offered to take us on a coffee tour. That morning I consumed more caffeine than ever, all in the, uh, name of science. As you read this, I might finally be returning to a normal sleeping cycle.

Now jet-propelled by coffee and pastries, we said goodbye to Ant and Toni and began driving northeast looking for those old cars and trucks.

We found some—in front yards, backyards, and open garages—but Seattle area folks wouldn't consider letting us interview them. Odd because I've been knocking on people's doors my whole life and never had *so* many people kindly deny my request.

We called Ant to recount our experience. He wasn't surprised. In fact, there's a name for Seattleites' reticence and low-key unfriendliness: the Seattle Freeze.

Defined as the practice of social distancing, the Seattle Freeze has nothing to do with Covid-19 avoidance. "Seattle, Social Distancing since 1953!" as one website describes it. Another post is more blunt: "Welcome to Seattle. Now go home."

The local Seattle PBS affiliate features *Mossback's Northwest*, a TV program hosted by Knute Berger. He describes the Seattle Freeze as passive-aggressive behavior brought on because the area's near-constant rain means Seattleites are cooped up at home for many months of the year. Knute's research has shown that, even 100 years ago, Seattleites

wouldn't talk to their seatmates on the city's streetcars. "It's a basic mistrust of newcomers," he suggests.

Which is exactly what I was experiencing. I'd knock on a door and start talking with the seemingly friendly owner of an old car or three, only to be told "no" to an actual interview—though they said it in a "nice" way. This happened whether the car in their yard was a Crosley station wagon, a big-block Chevelle, or a C-10 Chevy short bed pickup truck.

Frustrated, after a couple of hours we called it quits. I got in touch with my friends Brian and Chris Laine, who live in Arlington, Washington, about an hour north of Seattle. The Laines have joined a couple of the annual Cobra tours I host with my friend Jim Maxwell. Brian and Chris invited us to stay in their lovely home. Two nights in a row outside the Airstream!

Maybe our next book should be *Mooch Your Way Across America*.

The Laines also offered to let us park our rig in one of their car barns for a few weeks.

You see, in order to keep our sanity and retain some semblance of marriage with our very patient wives, real life, and careers, it was time for our month-long pit stop at this point in our adventure.

So hopefully your well-rested hosts will be full of new energy when we return in July. Or in your case, when you turn to the next page.

Top: MAR's friends Ant Matsuda (*left*) and Toni Pinto live in Issaquah, a Seattle suburb. We met them at—surprise!—a coffee shop. They advised us about places we should take in during our stay and explained the dreaded Seattle Freeze.

Bottom: My friends Chris and Brian Laine stored our rig in their Arlington barn for a few weeks. Brian is a serious car guy, willing to take on virtually any mechanical task related to his eclectic collection of sports and racing cars. We waved good-bye, took a right turn out of their driveway, and began the final leg of our road trip.

Top: Because Griot's Garage is one of Hagerty's marketing partners, they were eager to wash and detail our rig before we made it dirty again.

Bottom: Pro detailer Anthony used Griot's patented foam cannon on the Bronco and let it soak for about ten minutes. Afterward he used a high-pressure water spray to rinse it off. The result was amazing. Have you ever noticed clean cars always seem to drive better than dirty ones? Unfortunately ours wouldn't be clean for long.

RETURN TO SEATTLE

It was a Monday morning in early July and we had much to do. After our hiatus, MAR and I each arrived in Seattle from opposite ends of the country on Sunday evening and made plans to hit the ground running by 7 a.m. the next morning. We ordered a Lyft ride and had the driver deliver us to Brian and Chris Laine's house, about 90 minutes north of our hotel.

It had been over a month since our Bronco and Airstream had turned a wheel. In the interim, I filmed episodes for *Barn Find Hunter* in Maine, gave a talk at the Henry Ford Museum in Dearborn, Michigan, and did some sailing on "other people's boats." MAR had shot photos for *Porsche Panorama* magazine at the annual Porsche Parade, as well as completing work for his other automotive clients. We're both busy guys, so the four-week break had been a real blessing.

Brian and Chris had taken care of our Bronco and Airstream, squeaking our 30-foot (9-meter) rig into a 30-foot, 1-inch (9.1-meter) storage building. Brian kindly offered to wash our rig before we arrived, but we had other plans.

Griot's Garage, a shop known to gearheads everywhere and located in Tacoma, is a Hagerty marketing partner.

Company founder Richard Griot had offered to wash and detail our road-filthy rig before we departed on part two of our journey.

That afternoon at Griot's headquarters, their star detailer, Anthony, washed, debugged, and waxed both the Bronco and the Airstream, amazingly in just three hours. When he was done, they looked as good as the day I'd picked them up back in April.

We visited the Museum of Glass while we were in Tacoma. MAR had an upcoming Porsche photo shoot, another in his annual "Porsches and Architecture" series for *Panorama*, and wanted to check out the museum as a possible backdrop.

We were also scheduled to give a talk at America's Car Museum about our adventure up to that point—Key West to Seattle basically. Formerly the LeMay Museum, this Tacoma facility features an amazing range of exhibits. I wasn't able to tour the entire collection before our talk, but what I did see was impressive.

We had a good time recounting our adventures on the road, and afterward got to meet museum members and talk about their own automotive passions. It was a nice way to share the first 5,000 miles of our road trip, and begin recharging for our next driving stint to Alaska.

6.
INTO THE
GREAT
WHITE NORTH

WELCOME TO THE GREAT WHITE NORTH, EH?

Before I left Maine, I ordered a 2022 edition of *The Milepost*, a guide that's essential if you're traveling on the Alaska Highway through British Columbia, Yukon, and Alaska, or anywhere in the state of Alaska. The size of a phonebook, its over 700 pages list virtually every attraction, point of interest, gas station, restaurant, lodging, campground, store, and anything else you might need on every major road on the road to and within Alaska. Since 1948 *The Milepost* has been the bible for travel in the Last Frontier.

Unfortunately the order for the latest edition wouldn't arrive until we'd already departed for Seattle, but I could get a 2020 edition within a few days. I figured this would be good enough, as I assume things don't change that quickly in Alaska and that a two-year-old copy would work well enough for us. The book came in plenty of time, and I wound up using it as our mile-by-mile guide as we ventured north.

We hoped that we had our ducks in a row for the border crossing into Canada. MAR and I had exchanged several texts and phone calls about the special security requirements that have been put in place recently.

I've crossed the border to Canada several times in my life. The first was when some high school buddies and I decided to drive from Long Island to Canada for breakfast. Early in our marriage, Pat and I camped in Ontario and Nova Scotia, and then my son Brian and I drove my 1939 Ford Woody into Vancouver during our cross-country surfing safari.

The crossing used to be so simple—no passports required. Basically you smiled at the border guard, they smiled back, you told them where you were going, and they said, "Have a nice trip, eh."

It's rather more difficult now.

The 9/11 attacks made border crossing much more "official," with passports now required and sometimes extended questioning regarding destination, length of stay, purpose of trip, and so on. The border guards seldom smile these days —it's all business.

I understand the reasoning behind the increased scrutiny, but crossing into Canada has gone from a happy experience to one that elicits as much joy as preparing for a colonoscopy.

Before departing, MAR looked up the rules for entering Canada and discovered that we each needed to complete an ArriveCAN form. It required that we each submit photos of our passports as well as our Covid vaccination cards.

MAR had an additional challenge: his camera equipment. If we entered Canada with his cameras, lenses, tripod, and drone and didn't claim it all on the way in, then departing with that equipment might be a challenge. He might have purchased that equipment while in Canada, and they'd want the tax due on it when we exited.

He checked with other photographers, who suggested he register a carnet, a temporary import/export document that he'd fill out before entering the country. He was required to detail his equipment, including serial numbers, which would be verified by both U.S. and Canadian border guards upon entry and exit from Canada.

The bummer was that the document would cost us $600. There was a chance we wouldn't be questioned or inspected, but we didn't feel it was worth the risk. So $600 was sent to the carnet company and we held our breath that we'd be approved. I guess Canada finds a way to extract some money no matter what.

MAR was required to list the exact entry location, date, and approximate time that we would be entering the country.

WELCOME, MOMENTARILY, TO CANADA

We waited in traffic at the border-entry point on the Pacific coast for about twenty minutes before being told that MAR first needed to have his carnet stamped by U.S. Customs. We drove into Canada and with Airstream in tow, made an awkward U-turn, and returned to the U.S. side, where we were met by a very nice customs agent. In our attempt to reenter the U.S. the agent advised us to drive to another customs location about 1 mile (1.6 kilometers) to the east.

THE CROSSING USED TO BE SO SIMPLE. BASICALLY, YOU SMILED AT THE BORDER GUARD, THEY SMILED BACK, YOU TOLD THEM WHERE YOU WERE GOING, AND THEY SAID, "HAVE A NICE TRIP, EH."

Safely back in the U.S. of A., we had a little bit of time, so we did we always do: looked for a coffee shop. After MAR got his fancy coffee, we drove to the line at the second border crossing.

Shakespeare's *Much Ado About Nothing* would also be an apt description of our crossing into Canada. After weeks of worrying about the hassles, new border laws, researching customs requirements, completing online forms, submitting photos of passports and Covid vaccination records, acquiring letters from Ford and Airstream authorizing us to take our rig into Canada, we breezed through in a few minutes.

"Have a nice day," smiled the Canadian border crossing guard said as he sent us on our way.

MAR had estimated we'd get over the border at 10 a.m. Pacific Time. After visiting the wrong entry point, waiting in two twenty-minute lines, and loitering at a coffee shop, we crossed at 9:55 a.m. I love it when a plan works out.

We were in Canada, so we needed to adjust quickly to kilometers per hour, centigrade temperature readings, and really bad pizza. Eh?

VANCOUVER INTERLUDE

After crossing the border, we followed our *Milepost* directions onto Highway 99, which would take us directly through the center of Vancouver. What a beautiful city. We decided to pay a short visit to MAR's friend, Bob Styan, in the business district. He sells high-end real estate in the city's downtown, which meant finding a good place to park our cumbersome rig on the congested street. We decided to park illegally near a construction site for a few minutes while MAR and Bob spoke on the sidewalk.

As they spoke, I was struck by Vancouver's aroma. The ocean breeze wafting across nearby English Bay and passing through the trees and flowers nearby produced the most beautiful scent. I never would have experienced that fragrance unless we had stopped to visit Bob. It was a wonderful takeaway from our first stop in Canada.

NOT A NASCAR PIT STOP

Departing Vancouver, we followed *The Milepost*'s directions, remaining on Highway 99 toward Highway 97, which would ultimately lead us to the Alaska Highway. Out on the road, we came upon a woman lying on her back in the dirt under her vintage Ford Econoline van. She was attempting to repair a flat tire while her parasol-holding friend stood watching nearby.

Never one to pass up a fellow traveler in distress, I pulled over to lend a hand.

She was struggling under the van, wrestling to lower the spare tire, which has a rather complicated cable-lowering system that's invariably badly rusted. She introduced herself as Sully Messner. She and the van's owner, Arwen McDonald (with the parasol), had been on the road for several hours when the very bald, now very flat, tire gave up the ghost.

"We like road-tripping, beach life, and concerts," explained Arwen. They were headed to an outdoor concert and planned to camp in the van. Normally she would have taken her daily driver for a journey like this, but it has a blown engine, so she decided on the twenty-year-old van for the trip from their home on the Sunshine Coast in British Columbia. Sully works at an auto parts store, which puts repairing a flat squarely in her jurisdiction.

I tried to help Sully with the tire change, but it was clear she didn't want my help or advice. After about thirty minutes of providing moral support as she struggled with the aged rig, we wished them good luck and were on our way.

ONE GREAT ROAD AND TWENTY-THREE CAMELS

Highway 99 north of Vancouver is known as the Sea-to-Sky Highway because it begins on the shore of English Bay in Vancouver and ends in the mountains of the Pacific Coast Range. It is one of the most beautiful drives I've ever taken.

Highway 99 skirted the coast at sea level on our left along the brilliant blue water of Howe Sound while the mountains loomed larger on our right. More mountains, moderate in size and some with snow-covered peaks, could be seen to the north. Hours later, that same highway had ascended through switchbacks and on-camber turns to significant heights. It's the kind of fun road I seek out when scouting routes for my annual Cobra tours.

Eventually we reached the high desert with its farmland and pastures for grazing—even a vineyard along the banks of the Fraser River in the town of Lillooet, B.C. The terrain in Lillooet reminded me of Wyoming or Idaho, with a deep valley and roaring river below and grassy fields above. We crossed the river at the Bridge of Twenty-Three Camels, so named for the failed 1862 venture of John Calbreath, an enterprising resident who purchased that number of camels for $300 and had them shipped north from San Francisco. His grand plan was to replace the reluctant mules employed by miners during B.C.'s gold rush. The camels' tender feet, bad tempers, and foul odor scuttled his plan, but the lore surrounding his failure lent a colorful name to the bridge when it was built in 1913.

Above: North of Vancouver, we could see snowcapped peaks—in July! At sea level, however, the climate was much more temperate, in the low 70s F (around 20°C). Thanks for the nice greeting, Canada.

Winding up our first day in B.C., we found a nice little campground near Clinton and booked a campsite. It was late, approaching 9 p.m., but still light. We worried about finding a place to eat dinner, so we scrambled into town to see if anything was still open.

We found an open tavern featuring music at an eardrum-piercing level.

"We don't have buffalo wings, potato wedges, no French Fries, no hot dogs," offered the less-than-helpful server. Keeping it simple, we each ordered a grilled-cheese sandwich and whatever beer she decided to serve us and called it a night.

We'd left our KOA in Bow, Washington, at sunrise, yet when I checked our progress on the map, we'd scarcely covered any real distance! This was a big, big province, and traversing it was going to be more of a chore than I had imagined.

SKIP THE BOAT RIDE

It was time to say good-bye to Highway 99, which had graced us with some of the most beautiful scenery of the trip. At Cache Creek, we turned left onto Highway 97, also known as the Cariboo Highway. We would follow this road for the next couple of days. Initially this route had been fairly pedestrian, with commuters driving to work on a busy Wednesday morning, but the further north we progressed, the lighter the traffic became. We were now in the country.

Our goal that day was to reach the Alaska Highway, which looked to be about 10 hours away. Once on the Alcan (another name for the highway), we wouldn't make any course changes until we reached Delta Junction, Alaska.

I made a difficult decision that day: I cancelled our reservation for the ferry that would have taken us from Valdez to Whittier, Alaska.

I'd made the ferry reservations weeks earlier, while studying maps in my Maine cottage. I had taken it during the Last Frontier Cobra Tour in 2018, a great rally that only four Cobra owners had sufficient guts to enter. During that 2,000-mile (3,219-kilometer) lap around Alaska, which brought us from Anchorage to Fairbanks to Homer and Kenai, before returning to Anchorage, we loaded our four *real* AC Cobras onto the ferry in Valdez and for the next six hours were mesmerized by the most beautiful landscape I had seen in my life.

Pat and I are fairly well traveled, and we especially love the Alps that sit across the borders of Austria, Germany, Italy, and Switzerland with their snow-covered mountains and glaciers. But this ferry ride goes one better than a European road tour, adding a nautical element with crystal-clear water and the occasional whale. With this memory in my head, I made a plan that would detour us south for a couple of days so we could experience that passage before continuing our northern trek.

My plans were overly ambitious, as it occurred to me that, for us to reach Valdez by 5 a.m. on the appointed Saturday, we would need to drive about eighteen hours each day, bypassing all the beautiful sights in British Columbia and Yukon.

Reluctantly I sent an email cancelling the reservation. The cost had been $600, prepaid, so canceling at this late date—three days before the ferry ride—cost us a 50 percent penalty.

The cancellation lifted a weight from my shoulders though. We now had a much looser schedule where we could stop and take in the scenery whenever and wherever the urge might strike.

By the way, the Last Frontier Cobra Tour was where the great Fig Newton Fiasco that I mentioned earlier took place. My late friend Woody Woodruff and I had made lots of roadtrips together, and our favorite roadtrip food by far was Fig Newtons. So of course when Woody flew up to Fairbanks, Alaska, to become my copilot on the tour, he brought a package of the little fig biscuits with him. And everything was fine —we ate a few every day—until he forgot the cookies in my Cobra one night. Well, while we were sleeping in the hotel in the remote town of Girdwood, a brown bear, according to the State Trooper's report, caught a whiff and decided he had to eat them. So the bear ripped the convertible roof off my car and, with his huge muddy paws, reached into the cockpit and retrieved them.

When the media found out that a bear had broken into a $1 million Cobra to grab Fig Newtons within, the Bear Attacks Cobra story became one of the biggest "soft" news pieces in the world on that July day.

KEEP ON TRUCKIN'

My nose was constantly picking up the scent of old cars in Canada. All through British Columbia I spotted old cars in backyards, and the further north we traveled, the more I saw.

I told MAR that I would have to stop the next time we saw an old car or truck.

And there they were: some ramshackle old trucks on a commercial lot in McLeese Lake. I braked and made a U-turn. The small collection of vintage trucks were parked around what had once been a welding shop. A knock on the door of the adjacent house summoned Jerry Praslosk, the truck collection's owner.

BEANS & BARLEY

1444 102 AVENUE, SUITE 102, DAWSON CREEK, BC V1G 2C9, CANADA

Beans & Barley was our last great coffee stop as we ventured onto the Alaska Highway. I had no idea at this point that this my last cortado for days—I should have ordered two!

"I used to have those 340 Plymouth Dusters," Jerry said. "But if you got into drinking, you could kill yourself, eh?" Self-preservation led him to dump muscle cars and get into slower forms of transport.

To Jerry they were just old trucks, but to me they were examples of Canada's auto manufacturing past. To avoid high tariffs in the 1940s and 1950s, vehicles needed to be assembled in Canada with a high percentage of locally produced content. Simply shipping components over the border from Detroit was not sufficient. Canadian cars and trucks also needed to have brands and unique designs. The trucks in Jerry's side yard were a lesson in Canadian automotive history.

We checked out a Dodge truck. Well, it looked like a Dodge truck—it was actually a 1956 Fargo, a Dodge truck of Canadian manufacture.

"That one has a 354 Chrysler Hemi engine, and it starts right up," Jerry said proudly. I asked if he would start it, and he eagerly jumped into the cab, pumped the accelerator a couple times, and with a few revolutions it came to life.

I'm no Dodge truck historian, but I don't believe they were available with V-8 Hemi engines in the States but instead high-torque L-head in-line six-cylinder engines. So perhaps that was another difference with the Fargo brand.

Near the Fargo was a Ford cab-over engine (COE), the kind that drives hot rodders crazy. It sure looked like an early-1950s Ford, but it was branded as a Mercury. It appeared to be a very solid example, despite being seventy years old. Jerry referred to it as a "bubble-nose." It was one of several Mercury trucks scattered around his property.

Left: I always have an eye out for old vehicles, so we pulled into Jerry Praslosk's yard, a space littered with old trucks. This one, what appeared to be a 1956 Dodge, was actually a Fargo: a Dodge built by Chrysler Corporation in Canada for the Canadian market. I was surprised to find a Hemi engine under the hood, but apparently Hemis were available in commercial vehicles for the Canadian market back then.

Right: This Mercury cab-over engine was another Canadian-market truck in Jerry's yard. Mercury trucks were produced by Ford across the river from Detroit, in Windsor, Ontario, manufactured with a number of trim items produced exclusively in Canada in order to avoid import tariffs.

Left: Jerry Praslosk was a one-man comedy show, speaking with a thick Canadian accent. He gave up on fast cars long ago and now mostly collects old trucks and the tractors that people gift him.

Right: Welcome to Dawson Creek, the southern terminus of the Alaska Highway. This marker, the southernmost point of the highway, is in the middle of a traffic intersection and not really a safe location to shoot photos. We risked life and limb, dear reader—or at least getting a citation—to shoot this image for you.

The elegant Mercury trim on the COE was intact and in excellent condition. I can't imagine how difficult it would be to replace that trim if it were missing. Opening the hood, I found that the engine and gearbox had been removed, but when new it would have been powered by a Ford flathead V-8, probably of the 110-horsepower variety.

While under the hood, I noticed the factory ID badge still mounted on the firewall: "Ford of Canada, Ltd. Windsor, Ontario."

"I might fix up that old bubble-nose," Jerry said of the Merc. "I just happen to have a Cummings diesel in the shop with an automatic that would bolt right in."

Jerry was in the towing business. His collection included a number of tow trucks and flatbeds. "People are always giving me their old tractors, so I started dragging them home and I made a fence out of them."

I don't know much about Canadian humor, but much of what I do know I learned from Bob and Doug McKenzie, characters who hosted a show called *The Great White North*, which was a regular segment on the sketch comedy program *Second City Television* (*SCTV*). In a respectful yet hilarious manner, Rick Moranis and Dave Thomas (who played Bob and Doug) skewered Canadian culture with heavy accents punctuated by "eh?"

Anyway, Jerry had a Canadian accent as thick as Bob and Doug's, including the occasional "eh?" I loved talking with

him, and I wondered if he was similarly amused by my Long Island accent.

Jerry wasn't alone in collecting old vehicles: many of his neighbors had their own stashed Moraines around their property.

Why are so many vehicles parked behind rural homes in Canada? Mostly because of the low price they could get for scrap metal. Car owners have a problem: once a vehicle is worn out, there's no way to make money disposing of it. A vehicle's scrap value would be exceeded by the cost of transportation, sometimes hundreds of miles, to the junkyard. So there they sit.

For old car enthusiasts like me, rural Canada is the proverbial gold mine. As a bonus, salt is seldom, if ever, used on icy roads in this part of the world, so even older vehicles like Jerry's Mercury COE sport intact sheetmetal skins. Additionally the western Canadian climate is extremely dry, which means that snow often evaporates before melting.

I spotted numerous cars I would have loved to drag home, including a 1949 Pontiac Sedan Delivery, identical to one I'd recently spotted on the other side of the continent in Maine. But therein lies the problem: the cost to trailer a vehicle to the Lower 48, especially to the East Coast, would be excessive, possibly more than the car's actual value.

A possible solution might be devoting a family vacation in a motorhome dragging an empty trailer behind. Just a thought. (Tell your wife it was my idea.)

THE ALASKA HIGHWAY AT LAST

After two days of hard driving across Canada, we arrived in Dawson Creek, the southern terminus of the Alaska Highway. For all my five prior trips to Alaska, this was the first time I'd even touched the Alaska Highway.

It was Thursday, July 21. We'd pushed hard to get to Mile 0. But because we had canceled the Valdez-to-Whittier ferry reservation, MAR and I decided to take it a little bit easier: no forced marches from sunrise to sunset. (Daylight, by the way, was getting longer and longer the further north we traveled.)

We set a more reasonable goal of Fort Nelson, about six hours away, instead of going all the way to Watson Lake in Yukon, a drive that would've taken more than eleven hours.

Now on the Alaska Highway, north of Dawson Creek (but still on Highway 97), the road surface was acceptable and not riddled with potholes as I had been warned. Was there worse ahead of us?

We saw a small general stores about every hour, so finding gasoline was not as critical as it would be in a few days on the Dalton Highway. But it was lunchtime, so we stopped for fuel and food in Pink Mountain. Fuel was no problem, as long as we could find 87 octane. Gas was Can$2.16 a liter, about U.S. $10.88 a gallon at the conversion rate for that moment. Americans should not complain.

But food was another issue.

We could choose between those gas station rotisserie hot dogs turning forlornly on stainless-steel rollers all day long, or . . . well, that was the only choice. Hot dogs with relish and mustard it was. We went outside to "enjoy" our lunch at a picnic table.

While dining, I overheard a woman talking with another traveler about the run-in with a bear she'd had that morning. The conversation piqued my interest, so I asked for details.

"I got out of our tent this morning and went to where our food was hanging in a tree—hung on a rope 10 feet off the ground—and there's this big black bear!" explained Carol Wallace. "I tried to make myself look as big as possible, but he didn't back away. He eventually climbed the tree to see if we'd left anything behind."

Carol said that she and her twenty-one-year-old son, Curtis, had set up camp in the woods near the general store in Pink Mountain the night before. As dawn broke, she noticed food wrappers and other signs of human activity all around, which led her to believe bears knew the area as a rich source for scavenging.

The encounter amounted to nothing more than described: the bear went his way, Carol and Curtis broke camp and prepared for another day.

This was the first bear encounter the two had experienced since leaving their Billings, Montana, home *on bicycles* six weeks earlier.

"I didn't start long-distance riding until my four kids were grown," Carol said. Her first long ride with Curtis was on Route 66, "from Chicago to L.A.," as the song says. They rode about 2,500 miles (4,023 kilometers) on that trip. Their next ride was from Billings to Manitowoc, Wisconsin, across Lake Michigan by ferry to Ludington, through northern Michigan's Upper Peninsula, then back down into Wisconsin. That trip was 2,200 miles (3,540 kilometers).

Their trip from Billings to Alaska was even more ambitious. "It's about 2,700 miles from our home to Fairbanks," she said, "but we're thinking of going down to Anchorage afterward, which would make it about a 3,000-mile trip."

Carol and Curtis are some of the most dynamic people I've ever met. They traveled with what they could carry on their bicycles: a two-person tent, sleeping bags, food, spare tires, tools, and bike parts. They set up camp wherever they finished their day's ride, usually 40 to 70 miles (64 to 113 kilometers), depending on weather and elevation. Their home for the evening might be a forest, the roadside, or a farm field.

Exceptions to that routine were provided by Warmshowers, a nonprofit hospitality service that offers bicycle tourists meals, lodging, and a warm shower. Carol and Curtis are members, noting that there's nothing better than a Warmshowers host family inviting you in after a long day on the road. Unfortunately they wouldn't come close to another host on their route through rural British Columbia for the next 25 days.

At times they were surprised by strangers. "A lady in a grocery store asked us where we were staying that night, and we told her we didn't know," recalled Carol. "So she invited us to her house, served us dinner, and offered us beds. We've met so many nice people."

As I finished talking with Carol, a man who had ridden in on a muddy Harley-Davidson stood nearby, seeming interested in our conversation. He approached and asked, "Are you the *Barn Find Hunter*?"

I was stunned. An internet site said Pink Mountain was home to 100 people and 1,000 bison. And at least one bear. But a fan of my YouTube series?

"I could tell it was you as soon as I heard your voice," he said.

The motorcyclist was Jeff Mills of Vineland, New Jersey. He explained that he'd grown up restoring Model Ts with his father, and that now he enjoys them with his own children. He said his family watches every new episode of *Barn Find Hunter*.

Left: Jeff Mills from New Jersey, riding a very muddy Harley-Davidson, approached me in Pink Mountain. "Are you the *Barn Find Hunter*?" he wondered. We had a good time talking about Model As and Model Ts and about how he and his son enjoy my YouTube show. **Right:** In the tiny burg of Pink Mountain (100 people, 1,000 bison), we met the mother-and-son long-distance cycling team of Carol and Curtis Wallace. The two left their home in Montana and hoped to complete the 3,000-mile (4,800-kilometer) ride to Fairbanks before autumn. They hitched a ride with us to Fort Nelson, a couple of hours away by Bronco versus three days by bike.

"My friends and I go on annual motorcycle trips, but this year we went a little bit further than usual," Jeff recounted. They left New Jersey, headed west, and entered Canada from North Dakota. While traveling the Alaska Highway, they encountered a washed-out section of road and were forced to take a *400-mile (644-kilometer)* detour. We would soon experience that washout firsthand.

"We've ridden about 8,000 miles so far and we'll probably go another 3,500 miles before we reach home," he said. Ambitious.

It was then I decided that everyone on the Alaska Highway has a story to tell. You don't wind up here by accident.

As I said good-bye and good luck to Jeff and his friends, watching them rumble out of the dirt parking lot and down the road, a young man approached me.

Jadyn Dachuk, a twenty-two-year-old who lives alongside the other ninety-nine residents in Pink Mountain, told me he also watches *Barn Find Hunter*. How could this be? Here I was, at a very rural bump in the road, hundreds of miles from any sizable population centers (never mind access to cell-phone signal), and another old-car enthusiast had spotted me.

You could have knocked me over with a feather.

Jadyn told me he has a collection of high-performance trucks and muscle cars, including 1969 and 1979 Pontiac

Left: While still in Pink Mountain, local Jadyn Dachuk also recognized me and told me about the collection of hot rod trucks and muscle cars he and his dad have restored. I guess *Barn Find Hunter* fans are everywhere.

Right: Through most of British Columbia, this was the view from the Alaska Highway: stretches of up to 50 miles (80.5 kilometers) or so without a sign of civilization, but spectacular scenes of mountains, forest, rivers, and lakes. This is what most of the terrain looked like as we transported Carol and Curtis Wallace and their bicycles to Fort Nelson.

Firebirds, a restored 1969 Camaro Z28 ("except I put 20s on it," a.k.a. 20-inch-tall rims), and a 1974 Dodge Dart "powered by a 440, nitrous and tubbed with 25-inch-wide rims."

Interest in cars runs in his family. His father has a 632 cubic-inch (10-liter) big-block El Camino and his mother drives a fully restored 1973 Monte Carlo.

"I do everything myself, mechanicals, paint, and body-work," Jaydn said. The only vehicle Jadyn had nearby was one of his souped-up trucks, which he was eager to show me. It was a 1986 GMC 3500. Its 220,000-mile (354,000-kilometer) body was all that was stock.

"It has about 850 horsepower, if I can ever get it to run right," he said.

MAR and I had stopped at the town's general store for a splash of gas and a hot dog, or so we thought. An hour later we had to force ourselves to leave. I'm telling you, it was a memorable stop.

On the way out, Carol approached us and asked where we planned to spend the night. I told her a campground in Fort Nelson.

"Might we see you two there tonight?" I asked naively.

"Not likely," she said. "That's at least three days away for us."

Oh, right. Bicycles. I felt guilty. It would only take MAR and me a couple of hours.

"Would you like a ride?" I offered.

"You mean it?"

"Sure. We can put your bikes and gear in the Airstream."

It took us all of fifteen minutes to rearrange the Bronco to unfold the back seats for passengers. Soon everything was strapped down and we were on our way.

I DECIDED THAT EVERYONE ON THE ALASKA HIGHWAY, HAS A STORY TO TELL. YOU DON'T WIND UP HERE BY ACCIDENT.

On the two-hour drive, Carol shared a few more stories from the road.

"In Great Falls, just 300 miles from home, my bike frame broke," Carol said. "We were stuck there for nine days."

Her bike couldn't be repaired. She needed a new one, but even a used version of the one she wanted, a Surly Long Haul Trucker, would be $2,000.

"But then, totally by luck, I found one in Great Falls for $850. Soon we were back on our way."

Finding a place to sleep in Edmonton proved another challenge.

"We were south of Leduc and couldn't find a place to set up our tent," Carol explained. "We knocked on the doors of four or five farmhouses asking if we could pitch our tent on their lawn, but they all said 'no.' They told us, 'There's a campground down the road,' but I told them that would cost $20 per night and we just didn't have the money. Finally the last farmer said 'yes' and invited us in for tea."

Two hours later we pulled into the Triple "G" Hideaway campground in Fort Nelson and unpacked Carol and Curtis's bicycles and gear. In less than ten minutes, and somewhat surprisingly, they were loaded up and headed out. Carol explained that they preferred to sleep in the woods or public parks as opposed to campgrounds because of the fees.

Once again, we said our good-byes and good lucks, and the pair took off down the Alaska Highway, peddling to find a place to rest for the night—hopefully free of hungry bears.

ONE MAN'S JUNK

Because our schedule allowed for a more leisurely pace, after a visit to a coffee shop for breakfast that Friday morning, we decided to visit the Fort Nelson Heritage Museum, conveniently located right next to our campsite.

MEET THE BAC

T hat's a big-ass camper," I had said to MAR earlier in the week. It had passed us on a bridge as we were photographing our Bronco and Airstream. It passed us again later while we were pumping fuel. And it passed us once more, going southbound as we were heading north.

"I need to meet those people and see that truck," I told MAR. The truck, obviously from Europe, was like a large cube on a very tall 4X4 chassis. I hoped one day our paths along the Alaska Highway might cross.

Suddenly they did.

As MAR and I were inspecting and photographing rigs at the Fort Nelson Heritage Museum, I looked across the street and saw the big-ass camper (BAC) parked in the lot by the town visitors' center.

Fearing it might soon leave, we nearly sprinted across the Alaska Highway toward the truck. Nobody was home. I noticed "D" license plates, designating Deutschland (that is, Germany). We walked into the visitors' center and I noticed a German-looking couple seated at a bench near the front door.

I know what you're thinking, but I'm qualified to identify German-looking folks because I *am* one. My mother was from Germany, and I wore lederhosen for much of my youth. Really.

"Excuse me, is that your huge truck out there?" I asked. I wasn't sure if "big-ass camper" would translate.

"Yes, it is," the woman answered.

I explained that we had seen them pass us several times over the past few days and I wanted to ask a few questions about the truck and their trip.

"Go for it," invited the woman, Julia Stein, who along with husband Walter and their Jack Russell terrier, Wilma, were on the first year of a four-year around-the-world tour.

The Steins, from Schwaigern, Germany, had left home in summer 2021 in their BAC, beginning with a tour of continental Europe.

"People know Schwaigern because of our big church and very good wine," Julia said. Initially the couple toured Switzerland, Turkey, Romania, Syria, Italy, and Greece, but traveling became difficult as Covid-19 began closing borders. The Steins were traveling in Ukraine when Russia invaded in early 2022, which required a change of plan.

"When the war started in Ukraine, we didn't feel so good about continuing east, so we decided to go west," she said.

The Steins applied for U.S. visas and were inter-

viewed at the American embassy in Frankfurt. After five or six months, they were finally approved. They shipped the BAC from Hamburg by boat to Halifax, Nova Scotia. The Steins flew in, then began driving across Canada.

Regarding the truck, its coachwork was built by DXV and is mounted on a 4X4 MAN chassis.

Walter had been a professional equestrian who competed in horse-jumping events. He had used DXV-converted trucks to haul his horses across Europe. After he retired from jumping, DXV hired him as sales manager, a position he held for twenty years.

"DXV was primarily a horse-transport company, but they began to build these heavy-duty motor-

Left: Big-ass camper alert. The huge camper MAR and I had spotted over several days appeared in the parking lot across from the museum we were visiting. We hightailed it across the street to check out the 2002 MAN truck with a DXV camper conversion and German plates. It would be my preferred ride going into Armageddon.

Above: Julia and Walter Stein and their Jack Russell terrier, Wilma, hail from Schwaigern, Germany. The Steins were one year into a four-year, around-the-globe adventure when we met them. Their itinerary would take them through the United States, Central and South America, Africa, the Middle East, the Far East, and Eastern Europe before returning home.

homes," Walter explained. "When I retired from the company, we began thinking about a camper for ourselves. Julia designed the interior using a shoebox and cardboard dividers as walls."

Instead of ordering a new chassis, the Steins chose a twenty-year-old MAN, and for good reason: the mechanicals are more basic and repairs can be undertaken by mechanics almost anywhere in the world. The BAC weighs 8.6 tons (!) and is powered by a 6.7-liter diesel engine with 220 horsepower.

Walter drives and Julia navigates. When we met them, their plan was to travel to Deadhorse, then head south through the United States, then down to South America before shipping the camper to Africa.

"We'll eventually go back to tour Eastern Europe and the 'Stans," Julia said.

"I am confused," I confessed, "what do you mean, the 'Stans?"

"Oh, I'm sorry. Turkmenistan, Kazakhstan, Uzbekistan, Tajikistan, Kyrgyzstan, Pakistan, and maybe Afghanistan," she rattled off.

So with one year down, three to go, how are they getting along? "Our trip will take as long as it takes—or until our marriage fails," Julia said with a smile.

Below: Some might call it junk, but at the Fort Nelson Heritage Museum, vintage equipment like this Dodge A100–based snow machine reflects B.C.'s history all by itself; adapting a standard road vehicle into one built to tackle heavy snow. The museum is a collection of construction equipment from when the Alaska Highway was built, plus more current items like this 1960s-era Dodge.

Founded by a locally famous picker, the late Marl Brown, the museum displays include small, everyday historical items like kitchen accessories, hardware, clothing, cameras, and household items. But my interest was in the *huge* equipment parked outside. Much of it was surplus, originally brought to the area by the U.S. Army during construction of the Alaska Highway in 1942, then left behind once the work was done. I'm sure people in the area saw the rigs as abandoned vehicles until collectors like Brown began to gather it up for display.

Besides some automobiles, Jeeps, and standard-sized pickup trucks, there were huge trucks, bulldozers, graders, and a 20-foot-tall (6-meter-tall) engine, all assembled outside. The little boy in me was pretty excited. The Heritage Museum is like a countrified version of the Henry Ford Museum in Dearborn.

FRIGID WATER AND HUGE FRENCH TOAST

We've been driving on Highway 97, the Alaska Highway, for four days now and the scenery is astounding. The view through the windshield is almost too dramatic to put into words. What began with medium-sized mountains a few days ago has become the Canadian Rockies, rising to heights above the timberline. The color in the lower regions was a brilliant green from the abundant stands of evergreen trees, but the lack of color in the upper altitudes creates a sharp contrast.

The lakes and rivers are a misty green because the water originates from glacier melt, which carries minerals.

Muncho Lake, though, is crystal blue, the brilliant color a result of copper oxide leaching into the water from the shoreline. The color reminded me of the Meyers Manx dune buggy that fourteen-year-old me had dreamed of owning one day, in a color the catalog called Peacock Blue Metalflake.

We boondocked on the quiet shore of Muncho Lake at the Strawberry Flats campground. I attempted a swim in the frigid lake's waters, but I couldn't manage it. I was barefoot, and walking on the sharp volcanic rocks was more painful than I could bear. I waded up to my knees, but that was it for me. I dunked my head in and claimed victory.

I later asked a park ranger about the water temperature. "Pretty cold," he agreed. "Almost thermal."

I didn't know what thermal meant, but I imagined it meant near freezing. "Pretty cold," to say the least. Muncho means "big" in the native Kaska language. At 7½ miles (12 kilometers) long, 1 mile (1.6 kilometers) wide, and 730 feet (223 meters) deep, it certainly is.

Across the road at our campsite, we tapped into the small stash of Pilar Rum we'd scored back in Key West. MAR appreciated it more than I did, but it did offset the lake's cold bite.

Opposite: Here's a piece of equipment that fascinated me: a giant four-cylinder engine block used for mining and excavation equipment. I'm 6'3" (190 centimeters) and the engine is more than twice as tall. I'm standing next to the flywheel, which is lying on the ground, and on the right is the muffler. For mechanical geeks like me, this is very cool.

Above: We boondocked on British Columbia's beautiful Muncho Lake. Because we had some daylight, we decided to relax and tap into some more of the Pilar Rum we'd scored back in Key West. Not really my cup of tea, but MAR was all over it.

Right: I almost did it, and if the shallow lake had been sandy, I think I would have jumped into the icy, crystal-blue water. But the sharp volcanic stones on the lake's bottom made it difficult to walk in. I returned to the picnic table and the Pilar Rum.

A TRUCK DRIVER MIGHT BE ABLE TO EAT A FRENCH TOAST BREAKFAST OF THIS SIZE, BUT WE ARE MERE BRONCO PILOTS.

Our sponsors, Ford, Airstream, and Hagerty, expected regular social media updates, but in B.C. and later, in Alaska, we were often hundreds of miles from a cellphone tower. Wi-Fi in these regions is virtually nonexistent. We were literally "off the grid."

I felt guilty, but I also felt pretty good and very independent, being so disconnected from the rest of the world. Peace. No phone calls, texts, or Zoom meetings.

Each evening, MAR would stay up late to upload that day's photo files to the cloud. But that was out of the question at a remote place like Muncho Lake. He felt guilty about not being productive as we sipped rum by the lakeshore.

"Relax," I counseled. "Cherish this time and take it easy."

He's one of the most talented shooters on the planet, and he's always "on." It was a relief to see him "off" for a little while.

That night we went to the only eating establishment for at least 50 miles (80 kilometers), Double G Service. Not to be confused with the Triple "G" Hideaway we stayed at two nights earlier. There's no relation, that I know of.

Double G is operated by the father-and-son team of Jack and Scott Gunness. They sell fuel and some groceries along with operating the restaurant, a bakery, lodging, and a post office. But no beer. Tragedy.

Dinner at Double G was home cooked and generous. We ordered grilled-cheese sandwiches, each big enough to feed the two of us hungry road-trippers. I noted their breakfast cinnamon rolls on the counter. They were as big as my head! I knew where we were going to eat breakfast.

Jack and his brother bought the Double G in 1977. "We moved from Alberta, but originally we're from Ontario," said Jack. "The restaurant had been a family business started in 1953 when the Alaska Highway opened to the public. The original family came up with the U.S. Army, fell in love with the area, and stayed. Most of the businesses along this road opened in 1953 when the land was deeded."

Jack and his brother also ran a towing service and an auto repair shop, but it eventually got to be too much and they closed that part of their operation.

"We only close on Christmas Day," he explained. "Otherwise, we open every day at 6 a.m. We're here to feed the truck drivers. We feed them enough so they come back. We've gotten to be family after all these years. Tourists start to disappear by the middle of September. They're afraid of 'termination dust,' which is what we call it when snow starts dusting the mountain tops. Then it's just the truckers and us."

And the seven families who live in the area all year round.

"We have forty-two post office boxes, but only seven are used through the winter," Jack told us. "At one time there were thirty-five full-time families here, but when the highway was completed, they moved on."

Jack is proud of the food he and Scott serve, especially their baked goods. Jack boasts that, in his forty-five years of operating Double G, he's never sold store-bought bread. The loaves that come out of their oven are large, then hand-sliced with a knife that resembles a serrated machete. MAR and I shared an order of what is likely the world's largest French toast for breakfast. It's also delicious. A truck driver might have been able to eat a French Toast breakfast of this size on his own, but we are mere Bronco pilots.

Jack meets all sorts of interesting folks at the Double G.

"I met a British woman, a professor, who was walking across America," he recalled. "Her husband had recently died of cancer, so she was walking to raise awareness about cancer. That woman was fit!

"Another was a friend of ours, Roger, who made bread for us for a while. At fifty years old, he was having a midlife crisis, so he quit his job and dipped his toe in the Pacific Ocean. Then he walked across Canada and dipped his toe in the Atlantic Ocean. It took him about a year and a half. He never really went back to work after that."

In rural British Columbia, we'd stumbled upon this wonderful father-and-son baking and cooking team who only a few lucky people will ever meet. The food is so good, but the people and conversation are even better.

TROUBLE AHEAD

About 60 miles (97 kilometers) from Dawson Creek we came upon the recent Alaska Highway washout we'd heard and read so much about: a torrent of water had washed out a section of the highway earlier in the summer, forcing travelers to take a detour—a *400-mile* (*644-kilometer*) detour. Thankfully highway construction crews staged a 66-hour repair marathon to create a 2-mile (3.2-kilometer) detour around the washout site, an amazing feat considering the remote location. Highway traffic was again moving by the time we passed through.

When we arrived at the washout site, several weeks after the event, we waited only a short time for a pilot car to guide us through the newly constructed one-lane roadway. It didn't take us ten minutes before we were past the washout and on our way.

Later we heard that the washout was not due to faulty engineering, rather it was a collapsed beaver dam that loosed the flood, destroying the roadbed and pavement.

It's not nice to fool with Mother Nature.

7.

WELCOME TO THE YUKON TERRITORY

TRAVELERS ARE NEVER LOST

Crossing into Yukon brought an end to our old friend Highway 97, which ceded to Highway 1 at the territorial border. Since entering Canada five days before, we'd driven only two roads: Highways 99 and 97. Both were amazing for their variety of scenery and trail experiences. British Columbia is raw, natural, and sparsely populated. After covering more than 5,000 miles (8,047 kilometers) in the Lower 48—where one is never far from a McDonald's—it was fantastic to experience authentic wilderness. We'd occasionally pass through a small town, but otherwise it was trees, rivers, lakes, and mountains. If we parked on the side of the road to make a sandwich, the only sound was nature—birds chirping, a stream flowing.

Crossing from B.C. to Yukon wasn't a dramatic change—same terrain, similar road conditions, maybe a little rougher than in B.C.. We are still on the Alaska Highway, but we missed seeing the familiar Highway 97 signage.

About every 50 miles (80 kilometers) or so along the road we passed either a combination gas station and restaurant or, more typically, a shuttered version of same. It's a sad sight to see so many failed business establishments along the road. Most of the buildings sit forlorn with weeds taking over the parking lots and chains across driveway entrances. It was likely a far cry from the day optimistic folks moved to these remote regions to open businesses and provide services for truck drivers and adventurous tourists exploring the highway.

I imagine the families who invested their hard-earned money and effort to build these businesses here in the wilderness—restaurants, campgrounds, auto repair shops, hotels, and such—only to see them fail for whatever reason. I wouldn't be surprised if Covid-19 had been the cause of many of these closures. When the pandemic reared its ugly head in the spring of 2020, the U.S. and Canada virtually closed their respective borders to all but essential travel. For eighteen months, casual travelers, vacationers, and tourists were locked out of the Last Frontier. If these businesses were tightly financed or lacked cash reserves, I can understand why so many are now closed.

My hope is that, with an improved economy and the pandemic now under control, perhaps some of these businesses can have a fresh start.

Below: Life is good. This was typical of the scenery we experienced toward the end of our trip's Canadian leg. Watson Lake, located in the southern Yukon Territory, is one of the most beautiful locations we visited. A respite here helped us endure seemingly endless miles of dusty gravel roads as we approached the Canadian/Alaskan border.

"I WAS IN THE AMAZON WHEN COVID HIT, SO I PARKED MY BIKE IN BRAZIL FOR 14 MONTHS. I FLEW TO MIAMI, BOUGHT A [DODGE] RAM VAN AND BUILT IT INTO A CAMPER AND TOURED THE UNITED STATES. THE ROADS WERE EMPTY!"

TWO WHEELS TO ALASKA

We stopped for lunch and fuel in the rugged town of Watson Lake at Mile 635 on the Alaska Highway, just north of the British Columbia border. This town is one of those windy, dusty settlements that would like to be tourist friendly but is, well, windy and dusty. The town and lake bear the name of American trapper Frank Watson, who settled in the area toward the end of the nineteenth century after returning from a trapping trip in the Klondike. During construction of the Alaska Highway in 1942, the town was moved physically 7½ miles (12 kilometers) from the lakeshore to a location along the new highway. Today some 800 people inhabit the town, which is a transportation hub with roads leading into the remote Northwest Territories.

It was well past lunchtime. In a town of few restaurants, there were fewer still open, so we opted for a Chinese restaurant, the Nugget Restaurant. There seems to be a Chinese restaurant in every city in North America, and they always seem to be open and serving. Chinese food was not among our preferred dining choices, but any port in a storm.

Likely for reasons similar to our own, many other travelers chose to eat Chinese that day. Besides the usual assortment of trucks and campers, there were a number of adventure-style motorcycles in the parking lot, and quite a few riders downing General Tso's chicken and beef with broccoli dishes.

While we were eating, most of the other motorcyclists finished their meals and departed, leaving a lone rider at a table by himself. His dusty, mud-spattered BMW GS looked like it had already tackled the Alaska and Dalton Highways. As it turns out, it had.

I asked if I could join him and talk for a while. I was glad I did: Navot Borno proved to be an interesting and insightful traveler.

Navot, originally from Israel, had been on the road for three years and three months, having left his current home on the Pacific island of Palau in May 2019. When we encountered Navot, he had just left Deadhorse and was heading south.

Navot began his tour of North America by flying into Atlanta, where he bought a new BMW 1250 GS from a dealer. From Georgia he headed west and south, riding to California, then into Mexico. He continued south from there, spending time in Guatemala, El Salvador, Panama, Columbia, Venezuela, Ecuador, Peru, Argentina, Bolivia, and a slew of other countries that he rattled off faster than I could write.

"There's no road that connects Panama and Columbia, the so-called Darien Gap, so I had to load the motorcycle onto a plane," he said. "It's either that or you take a boat.

"I was in the Amazon when Covid hit, so I parked my bike in Brazil for fourteen months. I flew to Miami, bought a Dodge

Left: When we pulled into the Nugget Restaurant in Watson Lake, the parking lot was filled with at least a dozen adventure motorcycles, mostly BMWs. By the time we finished lunch, only one remained: The lone GS of Navot Borno.
Opposite: Navot was the most interesting person we had met on our journey to that point. Three-and-a-half years into a thorough around-the-world adventure, he shared his experiences of traveling through both rich and poor countries, and why U.S. citizens ranked near the bottom for their willingness to reach out to strangers.

Ram van and built it into a camper and toured the United States. The roads were empty!"

Behind his camper van, he towed a trailer that hauled—get this—another motorcycle and an ultralight aircraft. So while the rest of us were hunkered down trying to dodge coronavirus, Navot was exploring America on land and in the air!

"Last October I flew back to Brazil, retrieved my bike and hopped on a riverboat for eight days," he said. "When I hit the road again in Columbia, I was able to ride up the Pacific Coast all the way to Prudhoe Bay."

Navot had ridden his BMW 50,000 miles (80,467 kilometers) and was still touring Canada and the United States. When he decides there's nothing left to see in North America, he'll sell his motorcycle, fly to Africa, buy another bike, and begin another leg of his world tour.

I was curious how he could afford to remain on the road for so long. He told me he owns a successful tourist business on Palau, which offers tourists opportunities to scuba dive, skydive, and take helicopter trips.

"My wife and son are operating the business while I'm touring," he said. "I always take breaks and fly back home to my family. This is my road trip. My wife and I have already sailed around the world and spent four-and-a-half years at sea."

His overnight accommodations vary. He stays in hotels when he can, camps in a tent when he must. During the pandemic, many hotels closed, so he camped much of the time.

I was eager to learn more about Navot's travel philosophy. He told us about a man he recently met who had left Argentina walking with his dog and pushing a wagon. He had reached Yukon en route to Deadhorse when Navot encountered him.

"The world is divided into two kinds of people, the tourist and the traveler," he explained. "A tourist follows directions, but the traveler is never lost."

How about security? Did he ever feel threatened in places like Mexico?

"I felt safer in Mexico and South America than in the United States." As an American, it saddened me to hear this.

"In other countries, I don't travel through cities, only through small towns. I eat at small roadside stands in small villages. Because I'm a stranger, even very poor people offer me food at no cost because they're proud I've decided to visit their food stand. Around the world, strangers are honored and respected. Their attitude is, 'Tell me about yourself, and I'll tell you about me. Stay in my house, let me feed you.' Only in America is a stranger viewed as a threat. The rest of the world sees strangers as a source of knowledge. How is it that in a country where people have so much, they're so worried about losing it and so unwilling to help others?"

Navot noted that he was often chased off if he set up his tiny tent on private farmland in the States. Sadly in America we seem to be a "get off my lawn" country. It was hard to hear this.

I thanked Navot for his time and for teaching me a life lesson: There are no strangers, only friends we haven't met yet.

BARBECUE IN WHITEHORSE

The Yukon Territory is vast and desolate. MAR and I agree that this spectacular road gets more spectacular with every mile. As you can see in the photographs, Watson Lake was one of the most picturesque spots on our journey up to that point. With the Alaska Highway running along the lakeshore and a mountain range rising behind, MAR insisted we spend time here, shooting photos of our rig in both static and action modes.

My favorite image is the Bronco, with Airstream, blowing past the camera, dust and gravel flying. That photo captures the essence of our long trip: to follow roads less traveled from hither to yon. After dozens of drive-by shots, MAR signaled for me to park the rig and he sent his camera drone skyward for loftier images. For two serial road-trippers, the couple of hours we spent in and around that lake was pure joy.

The road surface, however, was less than spectacular—harsh even—so driving any sports car here, or anything with low ground clearance and low-profile tires, would not be fun. The Alaska Highway is the province of large, heavy trucks, and the route is gashed with ruts. So much for my Craigslist-Corvette-to-Alaska fantasy.

But for an SUV like our Bronco, this road and its scenery is heaven. In fact, the Bronco and Airstream combo continued to give us the best of both worlds: we were free from overpriced hotels, and we had the flexibility to call our own shots about where to spend the night.

It was Sunday morning, and we woke up in Whitehorse. The rapids of the nearby Yukon River are said to resemble a horse's mane, hence the city's name. Whitehorse is the capital of the territory, the largest city in northern Canada, and home to nearly 30,000 people. Settlers arrived in 1898 after gold was discovered on the cliffs of Miles Canyon to the south. Before 1942 Whitehorse could be reached only by rail, water, or air.

When we arrived Saturday night, it was obvious that Whitehorse was no sleepy burg, despite its remote setting. It was bustling with shopping centers, car dealerships, office buildings, and plenty of hotels, homes, apartments, and condo complexes. And restaurants with hourlong wait times.

Probably because Whitehorse is home to more than 1,000 caffeine-craving Yukon University students, the city offers a dozen coffee shops. Unfortunately the only one open on Sunday morning was the Starbucks—not our first choice. Over the course of our trip, we had come to appreciate the character, vibe, and of course the java offered by stand-alone, independent shops. Starbucks' corporate feel makes one's morning coffee feel like a clinical experience. But over thousands of miles, I had learned that if MAR doesn't get his jump-start cup of frou-frou coffee, Lord knows what sort of day may follow.

In contrast to our big-business coffee shop, we enjoyed a delicious meal at Smoke & Sow, a barbecue joint located in the same building as a gas station. The chef, who had launched his venture first as a food truck, took a different, almost nouveau, spin on preparing his shredded beef, pork, and chicken creations. It was clearly different than the North Carolina barbecue I'm accustomed to—and quite tasty.

Talking over dinner, MAR and I concluded that we are part of an elite traveling fraternity. On the road, in towns, at campgrounds, and yes, even at Starbucks, we are brothers and sisters with those ramblers around us, even if no words are spoken, or even if we speak the same language. Everyone offers a nod and a smile, code for "have a nice journey."

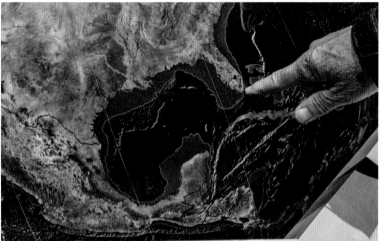

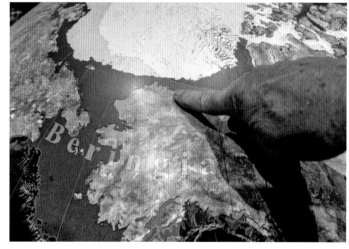

Opposite: Northwest of Watson Lake is Whitehorse, the biggest town we had visited in days, as evidenced by the Starbucks located there. One of the attractions we visited there was the Yukon Transportation Museum, which featured hundreds of examples of the extreme land vehicles and aircraft required to traverse the difficult local terrain.

Top: Taking a page from the World's Largest Ball of Twine in Kansas, Watson Lake's oddball tourist attraction is its Sign Post Forest. In 1942 a homesick U.S. serviceman working on the Alaska Highway, posted a sign noting the distance to his hometown. Today the display features more than 80,000 signs, and gladly accepts additional donations from passing travelers.

Above: You were here, and you are now here. One of the displays inside the Yukon Transportation Museum was a huge globe that utilized actual satellite imagery to designate land masses. I couldn't help but view the starting point of our adventure in Key West, Florida (left), and trace our approximate path across the continent to our finish line in Deadhorse, Alaska, on Prudhoe Bay (right).

I HEART CANADA

We've been traveling through Canada since we crossed the border near Vancouver six days ago, and today will be our last day here. We haven't been in any particular hurry, but we've spent four days in British Columbia, and this was our second day in Yukon. We hope to cross into Alaska today by early afternoon and into the town of Tok by dinnertime.

Before this adventure began, I was like many other know-it-all Americans, thinking of British Columbia and Yukon simply as territory to get through, a transit zone, en route to Alaska (you know, America part II).

No longer.

I am in love with Canada, its terrain, and its people. I will surely return and spend more time here. It feels like we've been traveling through a neutral territory that invites the world's travelers to come and enjoy the land regardless of whether they're passing through or staying for a spell.

Sometimes the roads are billiard-table smooth, sometimes bumpy, but most of the time average to rough, not much different than in the States. Not surprisingly, conditions got worse the further north we drove toward the border with Alaska. But at least there was evidence that Canada was making road repairs.

That said, we had been warned that the worst was yet to come. At a fuel stop north of Whitehorse, we spoke with a young couple who were in the process of moving from Anchorage to Missouri for a new job. Behind their pickup they hauled a trailer with their belongings. They were coming from the north, having driven the roads we were about to experience.

"You've got about 100 miles of good roads, then they'll get real bad pretty quickly once you enter Alaska," he said. "As Alaskan citizens, we're embarrassed by the condition of our roads."

I appreciated the heads-up. We continued driving north, while the couple continued south toward a new life. I quickly forgot about our conversation as we began looking for a spot to camp that night and a place to eat dinner. And scoping out coffee shops for our morning ritual, of course.

Late that afternoon we arrived at the Canadian-American border. As had been the case when we first crossed into Canada, MAR had to enter the Canadian customs building and present his dog-and-pony show as inspectors reviewed his cameras and carnet documentation. Then he had to repeat the whole procedure again for the U.S. agents. All told, it took a little over an hour to clear both Canadian and U.S. customs.

Once in Alaska, our pride about being back on American soil lasted about 2 miles (3.2 kilometers). As we'd been warned, the roads were *horrible.* "Pothole! Watch for that pothole!" "Oh, there's another pothole." And so on for at least 40 miles (64 kilometers). These were absolutely the worst roads we had experienced in the 7,500 miles (12,070 kilometers) we'd driven thus far.

Opposite: MAR and I achieved a milestone when we crossed from Yukon back into Alaska and the good old U.S.A.! Entering the final state of our long journey was a thrill, but I already regretted not spending more time in B.C. and Yukon. Often considered a "transit zone" connecting Washington state and Alaska, it is one of the most beautiful places I've visited on the planet. I'll be back.

Below: This sizable and interesting piece of equipment is the LeTourneau Overland Train. Commissioned by the U.S. Army as a snow-transportation experiment in the 1950s, the diesel/electric-powered vehicle measured 600-feet long when this "locomotive" was attached the other cars. As you can see, my six-foot, three-inch height doesn't come close to reaching the top of the tire.

The roads were bad, with seemingly no effort underway to repair them. I commuted on the Cross Bronx Expressway for two years in the 1980s, which seemed as smooth as glass in comparison. There were numerous signs of promised work—"Construction Ahead," "Loose Gravel"—but no sign of equipment or crews actually attempting to remedy the pocked surface.

I'm going to rant a bit here.

The Alaska Highway is a major thoroughfare for travelers from around the world entering the United States from Canada and heading into the forty-ninth state. And this ragged length of highway is their first impression of our country? This is the welcome mat we extend to visitors to the Land of the Free and the Home of the Brave?

This is bad PR—and I say that as a lifelong public relations executive. Down in the Lower 48, most highways along state and county lines have excellent road surfaces to impress incoming travelers and ease their travel. Alaska seems to have missed this lesson, whether it's the state or federal government that has dropped the ball. Forty miles (64 kilometers) of awful roads does not say "Welcome, we're glad you are here."

Rant out.

WHAT MAKES A TRUCKER TICK, IN TOK

Since the Alaska Highway is covered primarily by professional truckers, my plan was to corner one for a conversation before we left the Alaska Highway. We'd finally reached Tok, the first town of some size after crossing into the state. I hoped we could find a trucker who would tell us his story.

We wanted to celebrate arriving in the final state of our epic journey, and the internet identified Fast Eddy's as the best food in Tok. Burgers and beer, please. Packed with travelers and truckers alike, Fast Eddy's was the most crowded restaurant we'd visited since the Hogfish Bar & Grill in Key West some 7,500 miles (12,070 kilometers) before. The dirt parking lot was jammed with tractor-trailer trucks, motor-homes, trucks pulling campers and utility trailers, SUVs, and pickups. Clearly we weren't the only ones who'd read about Fast Eddy's in The Milepost and seen the complimentary reviews online.

As I was finally enjoying my cheeseburger, I struck up a conversation with the man in the booth next to us. Wouldn't you know it, he was a trucker. We spoke for a while, but because it was late and we were all road weary, we agreed to meet at his rig in the morning.

Jerry Fitzgerald is sixty-three-years old and lives in Hamilton, Mississippi. He's driven trucks since he was twenty-one. His current truck, a 2000 Peterbilt, has 1.2 million miles (1,931,212 kilometers) on the odometer, about half of which Jerry has added since he purchased it used.

"My father got me into reading Zane Grey adventure novels, which got me into dreaming about visiting the Pacific Northwest," he said. His father also insisted that Jerry attend college, so he put his wanderlust on hold for a few years as he joined ROTC and studied to become a fighter pilot.

"But the desire to always see what was over the next hill never went away. After graduation, I hit the road and have never stopped looking over the next hill."

We caught Jerry on his sixteenth trip on the Alaska Highway. True to his youthful Zane Grey dreams, he regularly trucks into Canada and the Pacific Northwest. "I think I've driven every back road in British Columbia and Alberta," Jerry said. "Once I had a haul from Whidbey Island, north of Seattle, to Key West."

At class reunions over the decades, former classmates always ask to see his photos and want to know where he's traveled. "I'm certainly the 'Most Well Traveled' of my graduating class!"

On the day we spoke with Jerry, he was hauling a very special load on his open trailer. "Right now, I have an F-18 jet engine, which is worth at least 5 million. This is a spare engine that I've been contracted to haul up to Fairbanks for scheduled maneuvers."

After dropping off the engine, Jerry will have twenty days before he needs to pick it up again and return it to Florida. "I'll probably go fishing on the Kenai Peninsula," he said. "The salmon there put up such a good fight. I'll try to get some of my family members to fly up and join me."

I was curious how today's trucking industry differs from when he first started.

"Fuel is the killer," he explained. "The government allows us to haul heavier loads to make up for the increased fuel charges, but it's really hurting me with all the money I'm putting in my tank. Since I've left Washington, I'm getting seven miles a gallon, which is outstanding. At times it's been as low as four miles a gallon." Jerry's rig had burned 261 gallons (988 liters) of diesel fuel since leaving Washington, which translated to about $1,500.

There are some amazing trucks plying the Alaska Highway, but the one that stood out in Jerry's memory was what he called a super load. "The rig," he explained, "was huge. It had sixteen rows of tires down each side, with two trucks pulling, two trucks pushing, two trailers long and two trailers wide. It was a million-pound load going up to the Tar Sands."

"You know, tourists pay thousands of dollars to visit a place like Alaska," he mused. "But the company pays me thousands of dollars to drive here. I call it hobby trucking."

Talk about traveling smart.

8.
FINALLY, ALASKA

THE 50-YEAR DREAM, REALIZED

Delta Junction marks the end of the Alaska Highway. It had been a wonderful few days' drive from Dawson Creek in British Columbia. At the northern terminus of the highway, we visited a small museum dedicated to the history of the Alaska Highway and the people who had built it.

The highway was constructed by the U.S. government in just eight months at a cost of $115,000,000 (about $2 billion today). From the southern terminus to Delta Junction it runs 1,422 miles (2,288 kilometers). When first built the Alaska Highway was 1,700 miles (2,736 kilometers) long, but continued tinkering with the route has gradually shortened its length. It opened to the public in 1948, initially as a rough and challenging drive, but now the entire route is paved.

Even though this was my sixth trip to Alaska, this was the first time I'd driven on the highway. On all my previous trips—three in the wintertime for the Iditarod, two in the summer for camping and touring—I had only flown in and out of the Anchorage airport.

Below: Yes, Virginia, there really is a North Pole! South of Fairbanks, is a year-round Christmas town, a major tourist attraction for families visiting the last frontier. A Santa Claus–house holiday store, candy cane streetlights, collections of children's letters written to Santa Claus, street names like Mistletoe Lane and Kris Kringle Drive, and a small herd of domesticated reindeer make this a popular destination a holiday treat, whenever you visit.

Left: I love old stuff—*all* old stuff. I dig old buildings, military and heavy equipment, and airplanes. The Fairbanks International Airport hosts a slew of old planes of all types arranged near the airfield. We spoke to one of the workmen, who told us they sell used parts to mechanics around the world in order to keep the aging aircraft aloft.

> "JOHN MUIR, THE FAMOUS NATURALIST, WROTE IN HIS JOURNAL THAT YOU SHOULD NEVER GO TO ALASKA AS A YOUNG MAN BECAUSE YOU'LL NEVER BE SATISFIED WITH ANY OTHER PLACE AS LONG AS YOU LIVE."
> — TOM BODETT

ALASKA DREAMIN'

My fascination with Alaska began in the early 1970s, spurred on by my older cousin Bill Cotter, who had recently moved there. To a teenager "trapped" on Long Island, Bill seemed to be living a life I could only dream of.

While a junior in high school, I went in with three friends of mine—Bob "Mini" Meade (now my brother-in-law), Bobby "Gonnie" Gallo, Jerry "Jeh" Bree—pooling what little cash we had to buy a 1959 International Harvester school bus for $185. Our plan was to convert it into a camper and drive it to California after graduation. The project kept us out of trouble as we plied our meager skills to build cabinets and bunk beds. We named the bus Stumpy Cloud for reasons that shall remain shrouded in mystery.

The plan was to tow the 1959 VW Beetle that my father had bought new (and I had converted into a Baja Bug) behind our converted school bus. Once we were in California, and after a couple days of surfing and people watching, I would take off in the Bug for a quick trip to Alaska to visit my cousin Bill. Like, for the weekend.

I had no idea about the time and distance required for such a journey. At best it would have taken weeks to cover that distance roundtrip. The Alaska Highway's unpaved surface would have further complicated the drive. And my vintage VW probably would have required an engine rebuild or three en route.

If I had actually made that trip, I would likely still be in the Last Frontier, either because the Beetle had met its maker in the wilderness or because I'd gotten a job on the Alaska pipeline and settled down.

But my friends and I started quarreling, and our cross-country trip never actually happened. We sold the bus to a hopeful rock band.

So in some ways, finally driving the Alaska Highway was the fulfillment of a desire I'd had a half century earlier.

Dreams do come true, but sometimes it takes fifty years.

FLEW WHEN PARKED

Once we left Delta Junction, it was a quick 100-mile (160 kilometers) sprint to Fairbanks. (Funny how, after about 7,000 miles (11,265 kilometers) since Key West, and 2,000 miles (322 kilometers) since Seattle, 100 miles seems like a quick trip to pick up a quart of milk.)

We opted for a hotel room in Fairbanks to recharge our batteries, literally and figuratively. We needed to catch up on emails and texts, and MAR could upload additional images to the cloud.

Checking around for hotels, I was shocked that even the Hampton Inn was $450 a night. That's a New York City price, last I looked. Looking more closely at our options, we found Sophie Station Suites at half that amount. Still expensive, but it wouldn't break the bank.

Lodging at the Sophie included other luxuries like hot showers, laundry, and some TV viewing. We also needed to post updates on Instagram and Facebook, something we'd been unable to do regularly when traveling off the grid in British Columbia, Yukon, and southern Alaska.

I was excited for dinner in Fairbanks: Friar Tuck's Hoagie House.

This is not your standard Subway. The owners have taken the hoagie/hero/sub/grinder sandwich concept to a new level. My son Brian and I first visited Friar Tuck's when in Fairbanks during our 2018 Cobra tour. The restaurant had recently opened, and I remembered their gourmet-style subs and terrific craft brew selection.

MAR was skeptical. Finally, in a sizable city, he was hoping for a nicer meal.

"Just try it," I beseeched him.

One visit was all it took: he was a convert. It became our second home for the duration of our stay in Fairbanks.

I had filmed some episodes of *Barn Find Hunter* in the Fairbanks area several years before, so with an open day, I convinced MAR that we should check out some of the finds I didn't have the time to investigate previously.

One area I wanted to visit was near Fairbanks International Airport, where I had spotted a number of older vehicles in and around the airport grounds. I recalled seeing a Chevy K5 Blazer with the optional factory camper unit installed, a very rare item indeed. Unfortunately when we returned to the site, it was no longer there.

I was intrigued, though, with the old aircraft that were stored there in an environment not unlike an automotive junkyard. Most looked to be from the 1950s and 1960s, but I'm no expert.

We later learned that, indeed, these were salvage planes to be raided for spare parts, just like in the car enthusiast world.

MEET THE MUSHER

From Fairbanks we headed to Nenana, Alaska, about 50 miles (80 kilometers) south on the Parks Highway heading toward Denali National Park.

Nenana is home to Cotters Sled Dog Rides and Tours. Remember when I mentioned my cousin Bill Cotter? Yep, he never left Alaska.

THE OTHER COTTER

Bill Cotter grew up in Milford, New Hampshire, the middle brother to my cousins Ann and Kathy.

We'll skip Bill's childhood years and jump ahead to college times. After graduating from Boston's Suffolk University in 1970 with a BA, he and a few of his college friends decided to drive to Alaska before starting law school.

"So, five of us left Boston in a VW Microbus," Bill recalled. "We were like five hippies, three guys and two girls, and just wanted to drive to the end of the road, which at the time was Fairbanks.

"When the summer was coming to an end, they all wanted to drive back to Boston, but I fell in love with the mountains and decided to stay. Plus, I was getting tired of them anyway."

With his newly earned diploma, Bill landed a job teaching history in a Fairbanks high school. After that gig he became a licensed electrician. Soon, work commenced on the infamous Alaska Pipeline, and he got a job that would last for a few years.

It was tough work: seven days a week, ten hours a day—nine weeks on, two weeks off—but the pay was outstanding.

"I was twenty-five years old and making $1,200 a week in 1973, and all my lodging and food was included," he said. "Most of the guys on the pipeline drank or took drugs, but I banked my money and started a construction company when the pipeline was finished."

Below: I'm lucky to have family in Florida—near the beginning of our journey—and in Alaska, near the end. My cousin, Bill Cotter (*right*), his wife Marlyn (*left*), and stepson Marwin operate Cotters Sled Dog Rides and Tours, where Alaska tourists can experience the exhilaration of being pulled by a team of sled dogs through the forest any time of year. The Cotters are joined here by Fairbanks, a descendent from one of Bill's early Iditarod teams.

Bill had taken up dogsledding in 1971, soon after moving to Alaska. He eventually settled in the remote town of Nenana, sort of a dogsledding capital of the region.

Here's a quick summary of his racing career:

- Competed in twenty-one Iditarod Trail Sled Dog Races, finished twenty
- Won the 1,000-mile Yukon Quest
- Competed in twenty-five races of 1,000 miles (1,609 kilometers) or more ("Enough to go around the world!")
- Iditarod record: six top-10 finishes, eighteen top-20 finishes
- Highest Iditarod finish: third place

Bill's last Iditarod entry was in 2013. Now 75 years of age and retired from racing, he operates a business that offers dogsled rides to tourists in summer and winter.

"One thing I've discovered: the internet allows you to live in the middle of nowhere and still have a successful business."

CAREER THAT WENT TO THE DOGS

It was 48°F (8.9°C) and raining when we awoke in our unheated Airstream parked in Bill's driveway. Cool, but my $15 Walmart sleeping bag, rated for 50° F (10°C), kept me toasty.

We spent part of the morning helping Bill, his wife Marlyn, and stepson Marwin feed and water his thirty-eight sled dogs. The cost to feed one dog for a year is about $1,000 because Bill buys the highest-quality food. That's $40,000 a year to feed the entire pack. Not a cheap proposition.

For someone from the Lower 48 who has only passing familiarity with dogsled racing, it might appear to be a cruel sport. But having spent more than twenty years around mushers and their dogs, I promise you it is anything but. Because of my cousin's involvement, I have attended three Iditarod races and visited Bill's kennel operation a number of times.

Racing dogs live to race, not unlike human race car drivers. The dogs wake up in the morning looking forward to being hitched up to a sled and put to work. When they're not hitched up, they are calm, loving animals who enjoy human interaction. When a sled appears they become excited, almost shouting, "Pick me! Pick me!"

"These dogs are my family," Bill said. "I've raised these dogs, their parents, grandparents, and great-grandparents. I know their bloodlines going back fifty years.

"The hardest part about raising dogs is when one dies of old age or cancer. I just never get used to it."

Bill told a story about racing in the Iditarod with the same lead dog he had used in a couple of the 1,000-mile races. For this particular race, the route had been changed slightly. Instead of the road veering to the right at a certain tree, it veered to the left. The dog knew every inch of that route so well, Bill said, that he stopped at that point, confused, and waited for Bill's direction. Amazingly intelligent dogs.

Bill occasionally rents out dog teams for major races, but he uses them mostly to give rides to Alaska tourists arriving on cruise ships. In the summer, he uses a custom-built aluminum cart with wheels to haul as many as nine tourists. He employs special multiperson sleds for winter rides.

"I charge $150 for a one-hour ride and $250 for a two-hour ride," he said. "The money is real good when I'm making it, but these dogs need to be fed and cared for even in the off-season, which is when the money gets tight."

Before we left Chateau Cotter to continue our quest north, we took a short ride in the summer cart. Bill hitched up Emmitt, Zeus, Zione, Birch, Sonya, Percy, Spruce, and Mikie, which left thirty other jealous dogs behind.

TRAVELING LIGHT(ER)

We said good-bye to Bill and his family, but it would only be for a few days. We'd disconnected the Airstream from the Bronco to leave it parked in their driveway for fear we might damage it on the very rough Dalton Highway. Even though the Basecamp 16X is built with off-roading in mind, I felt 1,000 miles (1,609 kilometers) of extreme terrain might be pushing it, especially since we'd be hundreds of miles from anyone who could repair it.

They say that if you have an issue on the Dalton Highway—run out of fuel, mechanical failure, accident, whatever—it's your own fault for not preparing. Being rescued is time consuming and expensive.

We didn't want to join that club, so we made arrangements to stay in traditional lodges for the next few nights. All of our roughing it would be in the driving.

RACING DOGS LIVE TO RACE, NOT UNLIKE
HUMAN RACE CAR DRIVERS.

9.
THE
FINAL
STRETCH

POTHOLES AND BUSTED WINDSHIELDS

Today, July 28, 2022, we begin the final stretch of our journey from Key West to Deadhorse, departing Fairbanks and driving north on the Dalton Highway to the end of the road, Deadhorse, Alaska, on Prudhoe Bay.

This trip has been a long time coming: a year of planning and preparation, solicitation of sponsors, and MAR and me clearing our schedules to remain off the grid—and away from our spouses—for almost two months.

Now it comes down to this, the final 500 miles (805 kilometers) to the end of the road, which will be mostly gravel, somewhat treacherous, and probably awesomely beautiful. If you've ever seen the show *Ice Road Truckers* on the History Channel, you'll recognize the Dalton Highway: it's one of the ice roads featured, only on the show it appears only in the wintertime.

We were warned to carry several spare tires, lots of window cleaner, and considerable patience. Oh, and we shouldn't be surprised if our windshield breaks before we reach the end. Since our windshield already has a stone chip we picked up somewhere around Alabama, this last possibility didn't bother me.

Cousin Bill told us about a mandatory pit stop at the Hilltop Restaurant north of Fairbanks. "It's where all the truckers eat. It will be your last pit stop for at least 200 miles. Besides, even if you're not hungry, they make the best pies in the state!"

Enough said. My Cobra-owning friend Paul Gould told me never to pass up a good pie.

We stopped at the Hilltop and grabbed blueberry pie to go.

The first 80 miles (129 kilometers) or so of the highway is paved but very bumpy. MAR is driving as I write these notes, and I hope I'll be able to read them when I transcribe these scribblings into a manuscript.

We are presently on the Elliott Highway, which is the "driveway" prelude to the Dalton Highway. Very occasionally we spot a house or hunting cabin, but we're mostly passing through a half-evergreen, half-hardwood forest. Most of the leafy trees are white birch, whose milky white trunks shimmer against the dark green forest when the sun shines on them.

The speed limit is 50 miles per hour (80 kilometers per hour), and we're pretty much sticking to that speed, partly because the road surface is so bumpy from frost heaves and partly because that's the speed of the tractor-trailer trucks in front of us.

Passing another vehicle on the gravel road might throw rocks into the passee's windshield, and the same thing might happen to us as we're being passed. We decide to play nice and travel with the surrounding vehicles.

HARDWOODS, SOFTWOODS, BURNT WOODS

The highway's altitude rose and fell, but it was evident on the upper portions of the Dalton Highway that the heavy forest was giving way to a more stunted variety of trees. This was probably due to the higher altitude's decreased oxygen and the extreme weather they must endure.

REMEMBER, THIS IS ALASKA, WHERE YOU STAND OUT
IN A SOCIAL SITUATION IF YOU DON'T HAVE MOSQUITO
GUTS SMEARED ON YOUR PANTS.

There's plenty of evidence of past forest fires in the area, most marked by a graveyard of blackened tree trunks. These used to be pine forests, but all that remains are branchless and naked stalks.

Some of those stalks, though, show evidence of rebirth, with the blackened trucks occasionally sprouting bright green fuzz. My unscientific mind suggests this happens if both the roots and the trunk internals remain intact and thus able to supply nourishment and hydration to the upper portions of the tree.

Anyway, that's the theory of this Barn Find Hunter who has zero qualifications for hypothesizing on the subject of horticulture, and whose only knowledge of trees relates to driving his Corvette-powered 1939 Ford Woody.

THE GREAT MOSQUITO BATTLE OF '22

Eventually that scrubby forest turned to ground-cover growth. Bill had told us that the terrain north of the Brooks Range would eventually give way to treeless tundra. "That's my favorite spot, but that's also where the mosquitos get real bad."

To prove the point, every time MAR or I open the door—no matter how quickly—some of those little bloodsuckers sneak in. Hunting them down and squashing them before they attack us has become our new favorite pastime, like playing punch bug or whack-a-mole.

Occasionally one of us will get lucky and pluck a plump one out of the air, but then the problem is disposing of the bloody corpse. A pant leg was usually the best choice. Re-

member, this is Alaska, where you stand out in a social situation if you don't have mosquito guts smeared on your pants.

Another mosquito extermination method while in a moving vehicle involves squishing them against the inside of the windshield or side glass. Methods vary between a closed fist or an open palm, but the results are always the same: dead bugs smeared on the inside glass, where windshield wipers and spray are no help.

We decided to leave their little corpses on the inside glass and consider it a form of abstract art.

BIKERS AND LIFERS

The surface of the Dalton Highway was 95 percent gravel or dirt for the first 150 miles (241 kilometers) north of Fairbanks. What pavement exists is far worse than the gravel. Again, my non-expert theory is that the gravel surface is more flexible and can be graded regularly after winter frost heaves, rain, and other issues. Pavement, however, must be scraped up and repaved.

We arrived in Coldfoot by midafternoon on July 28. I had read that Coldfoot was a rugged waypoint that offered fuel, meals, tourist T-shirts, and humble accommodations for not-so-humble prices. Essentially a muddy truck stop. Fuel of 87 octane—the only choice—was $7.50 a gallon. The station also sold diesel. The "restaurant" was an old wooden building that I'm sure could tell amazing stories about the people who have walked through its doors.

The lodging portion of the facility was across the muddy parking lot in a well-worn prefab building, which had once served as temporary housing for Alaska pipeline construction crews. As I suspected would be the case, it looked a little rough for my style. Thankfully, we had reservations at Boreal Lodging 13 miles (21 kilometers) north in Wiseman.

In the summer north of the Arctic Circle, nighttime is a relative thing, 200 miles north of Fairbanks. The day we stopped in Coldfoot, the Sun went down at 1:08 a.m. and rose again at 2:58 a.m., one hour and 50 minutes later. And nighttime was not fully dark, but similar to twilight.

There were many adventure motorcyclists in Coldfoot, some heading north, some returning south, others bunking in for the night.

Most of the riders were on big BMW GSs, others on KTMs, Yamahas, or a very occasional Harley-Davidson. Some riders were solo, others in small groups, and still others rode as part of an organized tour that provided the motorcycle, lodging, meals, and support services.

I spoke with John Palmer, a sixty-four-year-old from Middlesborough, England, who was riding with one of the organized tour groups.

"My initial plan was to ride from my home in the U.K. north to the North Sea, then into Europe, Greece, Turkey, Azerbaijan, take a ferry across the Caspian Sea, then Uzbekistan, Turkistan, and so forth," John said, rattling off these names like a college lecturer. He's not a professor, though, but a recently retired investment advisor who'd done quite well for himself.

John's plan came to a halt when Covid hit China in 2020 and nobody could enter the country. He had to plan out some detours to keep his dream trip alive. "I had my motorcycle, a KTM, shipped to Anchorage and here we are in Coldfoot. My original plan was to take three years, but this abbreviated trip will take about five months."

John is touring with a group called MotoQuest, which is based in Anchorage and Long Beach, California. He's ridden motorcycles his whole life, and this journey has been on his bucket list for years.

After talking with John, we visited the terrific tourist center across the Dalton Highway from the Coldfoot facility and run by U.S. Park Service. One of the rangers on duty was Heidi Schoppenhorst, who is also the proprietor of Boreal Lodging in Wiseman, our destination for the so-called "night."

Heidi has lived in this remote region of Alaska (250 miles,

402 kilometers, from the nearest shopping) her whole life.

"My dad was a bush pilot and hunting guide," Heidi said. "He bought the cabin in Wiseman when I was three or four years old."

Wiseman had been a gold mining center and trading community in the early 1900s.

"In the early days, supplies were brought up by either dogsled teams or steamships. Draft horses would also pull barges up the river. Later airplanes were used," Heidi explained. "There was no road to Wiseman until the pipeline and the Dalton Highway were built. It was either boat or fly.

Left: Retired investment advisor and motorcycle adventure rider John Palmer of the U.K. is riding his KTM on a worldwide tour of more countries than I could keep count of. When we met, he was on a leg that would take about five months to complete. Once Covid restrictions are lifted across China, he plans to be on the road for three years.

Right: Rarer than a Conch in Key West, innkeeper and park ranger Heidi Schoppenhorst was born and bred in Wiseman, Alaska, (population 9) thirteen miles (21 kilometers) north of Coldfoot. Her family's presence in this town predates both the Alaska pipeline and the Dalton Highway, back when getting to Wiseman required a plane, a boat, or a dogsled.

"When gold was discovered here, Wiseman grew larger than Anchorage."

In order for Heidi, her sister, and her brother to attend public school, the family rented an apartment in North Pole, south of Fairbanks, in the winter. But she was homeschooled in Wiseman after fourth grade.

Growing up in a town of fourteen people presented its challenges.

"I didn't have any friends," Heidi said matter of factly. "I had a brother and a sister. And an old lady, a nomadic Alaskan Nunamiut, who taught me her language. She couldn't read or write, so I brought over my storybooks and read them to her."

Heidi's father was opposed to the Alaska pipeline and the highway being constructed.

"It was so noisy with all the mining equipment," Heidi recalled. "And suddenly the caribou didn't migrate across the valley anymore. Workers came into Wiseman and stole our antiques."

Today the year-round population of Wiseman is nine, with that number probably doubling in summer. There are a couple of Airbnb rentals, a craft gallery, and a display of vintage mining equipment. That's it.

Yet it's a little gem of a community, offering the few travelers who stay a clean room, a soft bed, and a hot shower in the middle of a rather hostile environment.

THAT ANNOYING SPACE-TIME CONTINUUM

We slept like hibernating bears that night, but woke up at 6:30 a.m.—relatively late in the Land of the Midnight Sun. It was bright, sunny, and 37°F (2.8°C).

Heidi and her husband Scott's lodge was a great place to stay, the perfect alternative to the somewhat worn lodging we'd seen in Coldfoot.

This was a big day for MAR and me, one we'd been looking forward to since departing Key West in mid-May. We would reach the end of the road today: Deadhorse lay just 250 miles (402 kilometers) to the north. We would arrive there for lunch!

It was also my son's thirty-first birthday. When he was born in 1991, I wore a Maxwell House NASCAR Racing T-shirt in the delivery room. (Maxwell House Coffee was one of my clients at the time.) That launched an annual tradition, and I've worn that same T-shirt on his birthday every year since. Knowing

Above: This sign is a bit sobering, and must give most tourists like us pause while they calculate the risks and rewards of driving on probably the most untraveled road in America.

his birthday would fall during our road trip, I had packed the shirt in preparation. It fits a bit tighter now than in years past.

We drove back to Coldfoot for breakfast. The food there was special, again created with truckers in mind. Once you paid, you could visit the buffet line as many times as you liked. Last night the entrees had been pasta, meatloaf, and shredded barbecued beef, plus lots of veggies, a salad bar, and several desserts.

This morning the selection was pancakes, eggs, bacon, sausage, and on and on, as much as you cared to eat. Coldfoot's lodging might have been a bit rough, but its restaurant served the best food for miles in any direction. (Of course, it was the *only* food for miles.)

While eating breakfast we struck up a conversation with Jim Huffman, a driver for Black Gold Express, a trucking line that hauls almost exclusively from Fairbanks to Deadhorse.

"It will take you six or seven hours to get up to Deadhorse," Jim said. "Just waiting for and following the pilot car through the construction zone takes an hour."

No way, I thought, in my immaculate ignorance. It was 250 miles (402 kilometers), and I was a race driver. But Jim knew what he was talking about. Indeed most of the Dalton Highway we drove that morning, whether gravel or paved, was smooth enough to sustain a speed of 50 or 60 miles per hour (80 or 97 kilometers per hour), but two things held up our progress: the road construction, as Jim had warned, and MAR shooting photos.

Before leaving Coldfoot, we also chatted with Jerika Shupe, a young woman exploring the United States while living and working out of her camper van. She'd already visited Deadhorse, and she was headed south back toward Fairbanks. I felt she might have an interesting story to tell, but none of us had time for an in-depth conversation at that moment, standing in Coldfoot. We exchanged phone numbers and said we'd try to meet up in Fairbanks when we returned in a few days.

The scenery was spectacular on the northern half of the Dalton Highway. I hate to keep saying this, but it looked so much like the Austrian Alps. I haven't traveled everywhere on Earth, although my passport has been stamped at some iconic destinations. I can say that the mountains in the Brooks Range were simply awe inspiring.

It had snowed in the high elevations the night before, so there was a wonderful contrast between the peaks' gleaming white snow and the darker mountainsides below. Once we passed the peaks and began descending, we reached a place that's often mentioned on the news: the Alaska North Slope, the downhill slope that stretches from the mountain peaks to the Arctic Ocean. This area contains some of the world's largest petroleum reserves.

Once we reached the flatlands, we were on the tundra that Cousin Bill had told us about. There were no more trees and only occasional scrubby shrubs.

The road surface was periodically awful. Jim the trucker had been right: the drive from Coldfoot to Deadhorse was slow, tedious, and shake-your-fillings-loose bumpy. Every few minutes MAR exclaims "Jesus Christ!" as he attempts to negotiate the best path through this pothole minefield.

Initially I regretted leaving the Airstream behind in Cousin Bill's driveway, but now I'm feeling I made the best decision. That poor trailer, which has served us so well for six weeks of our trip, would have been beat to hell.

The road seemed to have achieved peak badness, but then a miracle happened: pavement appeared. Asphalt. Smooth and flat, as pretty as you please. If I closed my eyes this road could have been in Miami. From the worst to the best. Go figure. But for all I knew, it wouldn't last long and we'd be in pothole hell again.

But it didn't, and for the last 50 miles (80 kilometers) into Deadhorse, it was smooth sailing. Seemingly a reward as we rolled to the end of the road.

My theory (again) is that the road surface is left in rough condition to keep casual travelers from attempting the drive. Deadhorse is not a tourist town, and it's not prepared to handle hordes of ramblers seeking food, lodging, and entertainment.

Below: A stunning juxtaposition. Summer fireweed blooms in the foreground while fresh snow rests on the peaks of the distant range. Alaska offers so many of these visual contradictions, which is what makes a visit so rewarding.

10.

LIFE AT THE END OF THE ROAD

LAND OF METAL HOLES

We arrived in Deadhorse at 3:15 p.m., July 31, 2022. When we entered the "town," the trip odometer we had zeroed out at the southernmost point in Key West showed 8,881 miles (14,292 kilometers).

High-five. We'd reached the end of the road. Time to take a deep breath and raise a toast.

Having just driven on some of the smoothest pavement we'd seen since Florida, we arrived at a "town." No, really, it's a factory, one featuring muddy dirt roads and water-filled potholes. This despite the fact that the road is graded every day because of the huge number of heavy trucks and equipment that traverse these routes. We were truly a long way from the warm beaches and tourist-friendly environment of Key West, nearly 9,000 miles (14,484 kilometers) south and east. But for me, Deadhorse was more appealing *because* of its remote location and exclusivity.

THE HOTEL AT THE END OF ROAD

We may have reached the end of the road, but not the end of the story. When we began this journey, we arrived in Key West two days before our planned departure in order to get a feel for the area. We felt it was necessary to stay in Deadhorse for two days as well.

I imagine this is what life would be like in a colony on Mars: all business, no luxuries, but intriguing in a future-society kind of way. We had reservations at the Aurora Hotel, a large prefab metal structure that in Deadhorse might be the most attractive building in "town."

I write "town" in quotes because Deadhorse isn't really a town, it's an industrial site. It's not 50 percent industrial, or 75 percent industrial: it's 100 percent industrial.

There are
- Virtually no cars
- Many big trucks
- No kids
- No schools
- No stores
- No churches
- No pets
- No homes
- No restaurants

Deadhorse exists for one reason: to provide workers a place to live while they produce oil for the rest of us. Most people here work three weeks—twenty-one days straight, twelve hours a day—then they're off for three weeks, and they fly home at company expense to enjoy whatever it is they do when not working. We spoke to some workers who actually live in Fairbanks or Anchorage. Others live in Canada or somewhere else in the Lower 48.

Though I chose the Aurora Hotel randomly two months before from an online lodging website, it seems I could not have made a better choice. In Deadhorse, the Aurora is the equivalent of the Waldorf Astoria.

Like every other lodging option in Deadhorse—and virtually every other building—the Aurora is a metal modular building, its components likely brought in by ship and assembled onsite.

As you enter the foyer, a sign informs visitors that they are required to slip a pair of plastic booties over their boots or, in my case, Top-Siders. "Please help us keep the carpets clean," the sign implores.

DEADHORSE ISN'T REALLY A TOWN, IT'S AN INDUSTRIAL SITE.

Above: Literally the end of the road, Mile 414 of the Dalton Highway. We'd set the odometer to zero in Key West back in May. Here it turned 8,881 miles (14,292 kilometers) as we passed this sign. It was an incredible trip and I was sad to see it come to an end.

The booty requirement met no protests from the many, often burly oil field workers who made the Aurora their home for three weeks at a time. Once you get used to the fact that everybody wears little blue bootie covers over their shoes, it becomes second nature.

And the carpets are clean.

We began wearing the throwaway booties outdoors in order to keep our shoes from getting trashed as we walked on the muddy road.

We each had our own single bedroom joined by a Jack-and-Jill bathroom. The rooms were small, very clean, and offered the basics: TV, desk and chair, fridge, dresser. They got the job done.

In the center of the hotel was a large, modern laundry that required no money—detergent was automatically added, as it was included with the room charge.

Food was also included with the room. The Aurora offered many entrée choices along with veggies, desserts, sandwiches, and salads to cover all three daily meals—all you can eat, included in the $150 per night per person room charge.

Actually the kitchen appeared to be open all day, with a grab-and-go area where guests in a hurry can nab premade sandwiches, fruit, salad, drinks, and desserts before departing for the fields.

Diners are required to wear plastic gloves before entering the dining area and used throughout the buffet-style self-serving process. Like the shoe booties, there are no protests. The hotel is ultraclean, which is quite a tribute to the Aurora management's policies. Without them, and with the filth inherent in oil industry labor, this facility would otherwise be trashed.

Three days before I had checked the price of a room at the Hampton Inn in Fairbanks: $433 per night. And that didn't include food and laundry.

Further amenities give oil-field workers a sense of home, including a very nice exercise room, a game room, and a library and den with a fireplace and leather chairs overlooking Prudhoe Bay.

Guests are offered everything needed for a semicomfortable life—except alcohol.

MAR and I were looking forward to celebrating our accomplishment with a drink or three when we finally arrived in Deadhorse.

No can do.

The oil companies own Deadhorse, and the workers there are paid handsomely. (Laborers can make $1,000 a day, and all expenses are covered.) But for that handsome salary, the companies expect that everyone will work hard.

It doesn't take much imagination to realize that alcohol mixed with young men making lots of money is not a sustainable combination. Workers sign an agreement that they will not consume alcohol or drugs. If an individual is caught breaking the rules through the random checks the companies administer, that person is blackballed from all employers in Deadhorse.

It's rumored that years ago there was a secret speakeasy, but it was eventually discovered and shut down.

So we celebrated our accomplishment with iced tea.

RESERVATIONS FOR THE END OF THE ROAD

During our two days in Deadhorse, I couldn't shake the feeling that I shouldn't be there. I felt like I was doing something illegal. Remember when you were a kid and you snuck onto private property? It was that kind of feeling.

This industrial complex offered zero tourist attractions or comforts. Still it was a bucket-list destination for me. It's a cool place to visit, but don't even think about vacationing there.

We were in Deadhorse for 24 hours before we were able to actually go to the literal End of the Road. You see, tourists can't drive the last few miles because there are active oil fields, operating equipment, and high security. Those who choose to stand on the shore of the Arctic Ocean must make reservations 24 hours in advance, pass a security screening, and take a shuttle bus ride the final few miles.

I mentioned a trip I made with MAR, driving Route 66 in my 1939 Ford Woody. I performed a little ceremony, filling a plastic bottle with water from Lake Michigan on Chicago's eastern shore, then dumping it into the Pacific Ocean when we arrived in Santa Monica. When we drove the Model T Ford cross-country on the Lincoln Highway, we baptized the car's tires in the Atlantic Ocean, then again in the Pacific Ocean at the trip's conclusion in San Francisco.

I wanted to perform a similar ritual for this trip, so I took a swim before we departed Key West back in May and had hoped I'd have the guts to do the same in the Arctic Ocean. I thought I might chicken out. When I attempted a jump in freezing Muncho Lake a week before, I just couldn't bring myself to do it. Too cold, too rocky.

OTHER FOLKS ON
THE TOUR ASKED
IF I WOULD
ACTUALLY JUMP IN.
I WAS HONEST
AND TOLD THEM
I DIDN'T KNOW.

Top left: Water is always part of our victory celebration when we reach the end of our road trips. I didn't know if I'd actually have the guts, but I plunged into Deadhorse's Prudhoe Bay at the end of the road. It was cold, but not as cold as I'd imagined. Remember, I did it for you.

Bottom left: Went to the end of the world, jumped in, got the certificate. I was awarded membership in a very exclusive club: the Arctic Polar Bear Club. It will proudly hang on the office wall next to my Dinky Toy Club of America certificate.

Right: This is what victory looks like. MAR believed in my desire to document a journey across two-lane America and put his business on hold for two months to document it visually. A great codriver and a brilliant photographer.

But I was optimistic. I boarded the Prudhoe Bay shuttle bus wearing a bathing suit and my kayak shoes and carrying a beach towel. Other folks on the tour asked if I would actually jump in. I was honest and told them I didn't know.

When we arrived at the bay, the seemingly endless ocean ahead of me, Russia far in the distance, I decided to go for it. I would never have another chance.

Braving an air temperature of 39°F (3.9°C) and a water temperature of 40°F (4.4°C), I waded out and jumped in!

I did it for you, dear reader! I didn't want you to read about a guy who *almost* joined the Arctic Polar Bear Club.

Back on shore a fellow tourist dared, "I bet you'd never do that again!"

"For $100, I'll do it again right now," I replied. And I meant it, but he never came up with the scratch, so it was one and done, and I got the certificate.

LIFE IN THE TUNDRA

Back at the Aurora cafeteria, finally warm and dry, MAR and I shared a table with a couple of oil field workers, Adam O'Connor and Jordan Belcourt, both residents of Calgary. They work for Gyrodata, a company that surveys oil wells from inside the bore using gyroscopic instruments to keep the drilling directionally correct.

"It's a need-based service," Adam said. "If the oil company needs us, we could be here for a week or a month." They survey oil wells from Calgary to Seattle, Seattle to Anchorage, and Anchorage to the North Slope.

I wondered what life is like in Deadhorse, whether for a week or a month.

"It's pretty different," Adam admitted. "Everybody's always working. It's like prison without the bad guys."

Life can get boring for workers, especially if they're here for the long haul. Adam said he tries to stay in shape by going to the gym. And there are pool tables and ping-pong tables, but he admits there's nothing like being at home with his wife and kids.

"I wish I had had this job 20 years ago when I was 20, because it's tough when your wife and kids are waiting for you at home," said Jordan. "But I don't think a 20-year-old could handle the job. I'd say Adam and I have about ten years left to work for this company."

Adam originally wanted to be a schoolteacher, but he took the Gyrodata job because it pays better.

"If I worked my way into management, I could retire from this company," he said. "But the pay needs to be adjusted. We're making the same amount of money today as guys did 15 years ago. And like everybody, all our expenses have gone up."

Both Adam and Jordan said the toughest thing to get used to is the way the light changes from season to season. There are nearly twenty-four hours of darkness in the winter months and nearly twenty-four hours of daylight in the summer.

As we bid the two good night, Jordan offered us a couple of rules about living in the tundra:

- There's a beautiful woman behind every tree.
  (There are no trees).
- In Alaska, you never lose your woman,
  you only lose your place in line.

Thanks, Jordan, we'll keep these tips in mind.

Left: We met a couple of contractors who regularly travel to Deadhorse: Adam O'Connor (*left*) and Jordan Belcourt, both of Calgary. They measure the direction of oil well drilling, often spending long periods in Deadhorse and dreaming all the while of being home with their wives and children.

Below: Twelve years into what was supposed to have been a one- or two-year gig, Nancy Bremer works the front desk at the Aurora Hotel in Deadhorse. On duty three weeks at a time, Nancy admits she might never set foot outdoors for her entire stint, especially in the winter. But it's an inconvenience she tolerates willingly considering her three weeks of vacation for every three weeks worked, not to mention a very good salary.

Left: Key West had a large buoy designating the southernmost point in the continental U.S. Deadhorse had a rusty metal sign and a bunch of decals designating the equivalent northernmost point. I'm proud that MAR and I can now count ourselves among those few who have visited both locations. Where to next?

Right: I awoke after our first night in Deadhorse to find this big guy, a musk ox, sleeping against the building across from our hotel. It's a reminder that this land belongs to the wildlife. All the oil workers, truck drivers, and hotel staff are only guests who must learn to live with the animals whose home this really is.

LIKE A VACATION EVERY THREE WEEKS

Nancy Bremer works behind the front desk at the Aurora, though she lives in Boulder, Colorado. She's commuted to Deadhorse every three weeks for the past twelve years.

Nancy first came to Deadhorse when she was a sales rep for a card-based hotel-room entry system, a commonplace technology in our time that has replaced metal room keys. She was selling these systems to the various work camps on the North Slope.

"Ice Services, the company that owns the Aurora, started talking to me in 2008 about coming to work for them, but I was happily employed," Nancy said. "When I got laid off later that year, I sent them a note and they hired me. I thought, 'I guess I could do that for a year or two.'"

She said 2022 was a particularly busy summer tourist season. The busy season in Deadhorse is typically winter, when the tundra is frozen. Summertime temps (with highs around 55°F [13°C]) leave the tundra soft, which creates a hazard for heavy equipment.

"Tourists don't usually come up here in the winter, which is when we're busiest. Inviting tourists to stay here and eat here in the summer allows us to keep our staff employed and active year round.

"The good thing is that there's nothing to spend money on up here except the coffee shop," Nancy said. "It's a good thing I don't have this job in Hawaii, because there would be too much to do and too much to spend money on."

Nancy has seen a lot of interesting folks pass through during her twelve years on the job.

"Oh, jeez, there was the grandfather and grandson who drove their purple dune buggy from Alabama, one guy drove his Ferrari, and recently a man drove his Tesla up the Dalton Highway and almost didn't make it. But I guess the most unusual person was the man who walked up from South America."

Nancy's secret? "Some people work all year for a two-week vacation. I have a three-week vacation every three weeks!"

SHOPPING AT THE END OF THE ROAD

I wasn't completely accurate when I said there are no stores in Deadhorse. There is one rugged store that combines a post office, hardware and housewares store, and T-shirt shop all in one. It allows workers here to buy personal necessities like toothpaste and deodorant, along with duct tape and wrenches.

It's also the place where a rusty sign denotes the end of the road, a declaration that you have finally reached Deadhorse. We had to visit that shop if for no other reason than to take a photo proving our victory, the opposite of the southernmost point photo we'd shot in Key West back in May. I also wanted to buy a T-shirt, but nothing appealed to me.

Been there, done that, didn't get the T-shirt. Still MAR and I had just completed what would likely be the biggest adventure of our lives, taken a roadtrip that most people could only dream about. It was time to celebrate—with a cup of coffee!

11.
BACK TO
THE WORLD

A CHAT ON THE DALTON AND THE NEVER-ENDING ROADTRIPPER

On Monday, August 1, we pointed the Bronco south, having completed America's Greatest Road Trip. The drive back from Deadhorse was a calm one. The pressure to produce stories and photographs was over. We had driven this same road in the opposite direction two days before, so unless we could take a better photo than we already had, we could finally just sit back and enjoy the ride.

Heading south, we passed the same construction crews repairing and grading the Dalton Highway, a neverending job.

At one highway construction zone, a lady dressed in a safety-orange outfit with a stop sign in her hand motioned for us to pull over to wait for the pilot car. She walked over to the Bronco and told us her life story while we waited for ten minutes. It went something like this.

- She was born in South Africa.
- She has a twenty-one-year-old daughter, a twenty-year-old son, and a seventeen-year-old son.
- Her youngest son will enroll in Wyotech upon graduation from high school.
- She enjoys gardening and owns a landscaping business.

- She lives in a road-crew "man camp" with sixty men and sixteen women.
- She's tired of being hit on by all the men.
- She recently caught her husband in the garage having a tryst with her daughter's best friend.
- She is a substitute teacher at a high school where she encourages borderline students to work a bit harder so they don't have to repeat a grade.
- She and her daughter are going to buy a VW Beetle and drive to Florida, trying to touch every state on their roundtrip adventure.
- Yesterday a grizzly bear momma and her two cubs were watching her from the hill over there.

Thankfully the pilot car appeared and we were free to go. Sweet lady, but, man, she certainly had a lot on her mind to tell a couple of total strangers.

On our return trip we approached the Brooks Range from the north, which cast it in an entirely different light. The approaching mountains are beautiful from any direction, but somehow from the north even more so. The peaks were

sharp and chiseled in appearance. If memory from high school Earth science class serves me, these are new mountains, not yet worn down by erosion, glaciers, and time.

The Dalton Highway changed from rough gravel to asphalt to smooth gravel, then back again. When the gravel was smooth, I paid no attention to the speed limit, which is 50 miles per hour (80 kilometers per hour). I mean, there was probably no other car anywhere near us—except for that one Alaska State Trooper with his radar gun.

"You were doing 70 in a 50 mile-per-hour zone," he informed me.

I told him I was so happy to be back on smooth pavement, I wasn't paying attention to my speed.

"I understand," he said, but I don't think he did because he then asked for my license, insurance document, and registration papers. I told him the vehicle belonged to Ford Motor Company, not me. He asked if we were part of vehicle testing, which is something that auto companies do on the Dalton.

"No, we're writing a book."

He walked behind his vehicle and used his satellite phone, probably to call headquarters. He was gone about ten minutes.

"THERE'S SO MUCH TO DISCOVER ON THE ROAD, BUT MOST PEOPLE WILL NEVER FIND OUT BECAUSE THEY NEVER LEAVE THE PORCH."

When he returned to my open window, he handed back the paperwork and told me to keep the speed limit in mind.

"That's it, no ticket?" I asked

"Not this time," he warned.

"Thank you!" and I shook his hand.

We'd driven 9,000 miles (14,484 kilometers)—and no tickets!

ALASKA TRAVELER QUIZ

The drive south from Deadhorse allowed for reflection on where we'd just been.

Boring people generally don't travel to Alaska's outback. Everyone we had met coming up the Alaska Highway and driving on the Dalton Highway led interesting lives and had interesting stories to tell.

Today when travel experiences can be packaged and purchased with the click of a few buttons, there are still folks who want to do it the old-fashioned way. Driving north of Fairbanks on the Dalton Highway is not easy. It takes a fair amount of effort to travel there, and tourists must be prepared for some level of discomfort: bumpy roads, less-than-five-star lodging (but five-star price), dirt, mosquitoes. But for a traveler in rural Alaska, these are simply speed bumps en route to a unique life experience.

To ensure that the Last Frontier does not become some sort of overrun Disney World, I've come up with a simple quiz for would-be visitors.

- *Do you mind getting dirty?* Dirt, mud, and dust are an Alaskan way of life.
- *Do you hate mosquitoes?* These bloodsucking pests are part of a healthy ecosystem, and part of the food chain. Mosquitos are a way of life here.
- *Do you want to lose weight?* Truck stops, often the only place to eat, want to keep truckers happy by offering large amounts of flavorful foods. All-you-can-eat dining is standard.

If you answer yes to any of these questions, consider staying home.

THE ENDLESS ROAD TRIP

We had met an interesting woman several days before in Coldfoot and decided we would try to pick up our conversation when we caught up with her in Fairbanks. Thirty-year-old Jerika Shupe met us at the Fountainhead Museum. After my talk we sat down to visit.

"I'm originally from North Ogden, Utah, but have been living the Van Life on and off for seven years," Jerika said. "I live full-time in my van, a converted Dodge Ram ProMaster, and I don't even own a house."

As a professional business coach, Jerika just might have the ideal career for her nonstop life on the road. "It's all virtual. I help people grow their businesses through actions and mindset. But believe it or not, I studied theater in school.

"When I started this Van Life, I was married. Originally when my husband and I had the opportunity to live on the road, we declined. But eventually we bought a minivan and loved the life. It was so different from anything we'd ever done before. So we bought this converted Dodge van, which was larger. But we got divorced a year later."

Jerika has continued life on the road solo. She's traveled throughout the United States, with only five states left to visit to complete her tour of the entire country.

"Alaska and the Dalton Highway was a big stretch for me. I was intimidated, but I loved it. I stayed in Deadhorse for two days, found a Wi-Fi signal, and just worked away surrounded by tundra.

"There's so much to discover on the road, but most people will never find out because they never leave the porch."

Jerika has a ritual that helps her make new friends. "I go to church every week wherever I am. People in church often invite me to their homes for a meal. Strangers become friends.

"I'll keep going with this lifestyle until I have a good reason to stop. And right now, I don't have a reason to stop."

Of all the travelers we had met along our journey from Key West to Deadhorse, Jerika stood out. She was not on a two-week or one-year or even a four-year vacation, but was on the road for life. No time limits. The road was her neighborhood, its inhabitants her family.

Something inside me clicked. This woman had it right, through a combination of the spirit of adventure and the flexibility of an online career.

We could all learn something from Jerika.

After the Fountainhead presentation and interviewing Jerika, it was off to Cousin Bill's to retrieve our Airstream. After eight weeks of off-the-grid camping, this would be our last night we'd spend in the trailer.

Top: The museum specializes in pre–World War II and Brass Era cars. The museum owns two Duesenbergs, including this 1931 supercharged Duesenberg Model SJ, one of the prizes in the collection.

Middle: Willy Vinton, seated here in a 1911 Everett, has transformed the Fountainhead Museum from a building full of cars into a destination for car enthusiasts and tourists alike. He regularly ships cars to events in the Lower 48, where they have won awards at shows such as the Amelia Island Concours d'Elegance in Florida. Plans for the future include doubling the size of the building.

Bottom: Back in Fairbanks, I was invited to give a talk about barn finding at the Fountainhead Auto Museum. Its world-class collection of cars and period clothing is one of the top tourist attractions in the city, according to TripAdvisor, even attracting many nonenthusiasts.

THE LAST CAR MUSEUM IN THE FINAL FRONTIER

I made friends with Willy Vinton several years ago when I organized the Last Frontier Cobra Tour with three other adventurous Cobra owners. Willy, who's seventy-four years old, is museum manager of the Fountainhead Antique Auto Museum in downtown Fairbanks. I don't think most people travel to Alaska seeking antique cars, but the Fountainhead Museum offers a world-class collection of early cars and vintage clothing. It's really quite effective and draws in tourists who are not necessarily car enthusiasts. Tripadvisor rates it the #1 Tourist Attraction in Fairbanks.

The last time I was in Fairbanks, during the Cobra tour, Willy allowed me to use the museum's shop to fiddle with my Cobra's clutch, which had been giving me problems. On this trip I promised Willy I would stop by on our return from Deadhorse to give a presentation called "Stories of the Barn Find Hunter" to his museum members.

Willy moved from Montana to Alaska forty years ago and now considers himself a Sourdough (a person who spends an entire winter season north of the Arctic Circle).

"I moved when the economy started to go down in Montana, and I opened an auto repair shop here," Willy said. "Then I opened a Peterbilt truck dealership. When I sold that, I was told about an antique car museum was about to open in Fairbanks, and owner Tim Cerny offered me a job in 2007. I haven't left yet."

Willy said most people visiting the museum are not serious car enthusiasts, simply tourists exploring Fairbanks. "Our fashion displays attract a lot of people. If we have a 1910 car on display, we'll display clothing next to the car from that era. We have more women's clothing because you can still find it. Most men's clothing gets worn out and doesn't survive."

He's proud of the recognition the museum has received throughout the United States. "We've shown cars at Amelia Island twice and won Best of Class for our 1932 Cadillac." The museum display space is maxed out with seventy-seven cars.

"Our plan is to grow," Willy said. "We currently have 30,000 square feet, and we're talking about either adding another 30,000 square feet or just putting up a much larger building."

MISSED IN A SEA OF ALUMINUM

Our last night of camping was at the Riverside RV campground in North Pole near Fairbanks. Coincidentally there was an Airstream convention going on at the same campground. Thirty Airstream trailers of all styles and vintages were in attendance, pulled by trucks with license plates from New Mexico, California, Michigan, Alabama, Texas, Virginia, Georgia, Ohio, North Carolina, Washington, Oregon, Arizona, Minnesota, Nebraska, and British Columbia. Interestingly all the trailers were traditional Airstreams, not a single Basecamp like ours.

I awoke the next morning anxious to swap Airstream stories, only to find all the convention campers rolling out of the parking lot on a tour bus headed to Fairbanks.

Left: I met Nick Brischler's father, Buzzy, in third grade. I was introduced to trailer camping when Buzzy's parents invited me to join them on a camping trip. I reconnected with Nick in Fairbanks, where he's a helicopter pilot stationed with the U.S. Army. Interestingly he and his wife Julia are planning to purchase a Bronco and Airstream Basecamp like our rig.
Below: Jerika Shupe's home is the road. She's lived on and off inside a converted van for seven years. Blessed with a consulting job that allows her to work wherever she has a Wi-Fi signal, Jerika has traveled to nearly every state in the continental United States, most recently traveling up to Coldfoot and Deadhorse.
Right: Of course, we met Nick at Friar Tuck's, a favorite Fairbanks watering hole. Their selection of coffee isn't worth writing about (sorry MAR), but their local craft-brew selection is the best.

ALASKA COFFEE ROASTERS

WEST VALLEY PLAZA, 4001 GEIST ROAD, SUITE 6, 4001 GEIST RD #1&2, FAIRBANKS, AK 99709

If you're in Fairbanks and heading north from there, then stop for coffee up at Alaska Coffee Roasters. It's a great locals hangout, and it's the last serious coffee shop from there to the Arctic Circle. We had the good fortune to enjoy it on both ends of our final stretch to Deadhorse. It was also our final cup of coffee together at the end of our entire trip.

"A JOURNEY IS A PERSON IN ITSELF; NO TWO ARE ALIKE. AND ALL PLANS, SAFEGUARDS, POLICING, AND COERCION ARE FRUITLESS... WE DO NOT TAKE A TRIP; A TRIP TAKES US."
— JOHN STEINBECK, *TRAVELS WITH CHARLEY*

FULL CIRCLE

Before we flew home, I wanted to connect with Nick Brischler. Nick grew up in San Diego intrigued by the military aircraft that flew over his house every day.

"I'd watch war movies with my father and grandfather, and I really fell in love with the military. I struggled with whether to go into the car business—because, like my dad, I love cars—or the military. When I was offered a four-year college scholarship if I joined the army, that sealed the deal."

Nick earned his bachelor's degree at the University of California, Santa Barbara. He is an Apache helicopter pilot and has been stationed in Alabama, Germany, and now Fairbanks. Along the line, he married Julia, "the girl I had a crush on in second grade."

"I love Alaska," Nick enthused. "If there was a way for me to remain in Alaska after my military career, I think I would. I love flying and could see myself piloting a floatplane."

Let me explain why I was eager to meet with Nick. Near the beginning of this road-trip tale, I mentioned that, when I was twelve years old, friends had invited me to camp in their trailer. It was my first and, until this Key West–to–Deadhorse expedition, my only camping trailer experience. I reflected on that trip many times during this road trip.

The friend who invited me on that trip, some fifty-five years ago, was Nick's father Charles Brischler—my childhood friend Buzzy.

Sometimes it takes fifty years to come full circle. When Nick's grandparents invited me to camp with their family, it gave me a wanderlust that I've never shaken. What's over that hill, around the next corner? How long would it take to drive from here to there?

My life has been one long road trip. I've been satisfied with my station in life, yes, but always curious about what's next. When a bicycle was my transport, I always rode further from home than my parents would have preferred. When I got my driver's license, I was on the road whenever I wasn't in school or working. Fifty years later, not much has changed. And now I've just completed the longest point-to-point drive in North America.

Seeing the landmarks and scenery, though, is only half the pleasure. Meeting the people along the way—people who might look different than me, who might think differently than me, whether I meet them in Tok, Alaska, or Venice, Florida—meeting them is the true joy of travel.

In the process of driving nearly 9,000 miles (14,484 kilometers), I met dozens of people ranging from restaurant servers to cowboys to fellow travelers, families moving to find a better life and others who never wanted to settle down. Despite what we might hear in the news or read on social media, the folks I met were more interested in getting their crops harvested or taking care of their families, or, like me, wondering what made other people tick. Nobody I met preached about their political beliefs or complained about the noise amplified daily by the media.

There is more to unite us than there is to divide us. All you need to do is leave your porch for proof. See you on the road.

INDEX

*Page numbers in **bold** type indicate images*

Quarto.com

2023 Quarto Publishing Group USA inc.
Text © 2023 Tom Cotter
Photography © 2023 Michael Alan Ross

First published in 2023 by Motorbooks, an imprint of the Quarto Group,
100 Cummings Center, Suite 265-D, Beverly, MA 01915, USA.
T (978) 282-9590 f (978) 283-2742

Motorbooks titles are also available at discount for retail, wholesale, promotional, and bulk purchase. For details, contact the special sales manager by email at specialsales@quarto.com or by mail at the Quarto Group, attn: Special Sales Manager, 100 Cummings Center, Suite 265-D, Beverly, MA 01915, USA.

27 26 25 24 23   1 2 3 4 5

Isbn: 978-0-7603-8106-9

Digital edition published in 2023
Eisbn: 978-0-7603-8107-6

Library of Congress cataloging-in-publication data

Names: Cotter, Tom, 1954- author. I Ross, Michael Alan, photographer.
Title: *America's Greatest Road Trip: Key West to Deadhorse: 9,000 miles Across Backroad USA* / Tom Cotter; photography by Michael Alan Ross.
Other titles: *Key West to Deadhorse: 9,000 Miles Across Backroad USA*
Description: Beverly, MA: Motorbooks, 2023. I Includes index. I Summary: "Tom Cotter undertakes his most epic adventure in America's Greatest Road Trip. Launching from Key West, Florida, Cotter and photographer Michael Alan Ross pilot their Ford Bronco/Airstream camper combination nearly 9,000 miles to America's literal end of the road in Deadhorse, Alaska"--Provided by publisher.
Identifiers: LCCN 2023006883 I ISBN 9780760381069 I ISBN 9780760381076 (ebook)
Subjects: LCSH: Cotter, Tom, 1954---Travel--United States. I Ross, Michael Alan--Travel--United States. I United States--Description and travel. I Automobile travel--United States. I Airstream trailers.
Classification: LCC E169.Z83 C678 2023 I DDC 917.304--dc23/eng/20230223
LC record available at https://lccn.loc.gov/2023006883

Design and layout: Justin Page

Printed in China